the Truuuly Scrumptious

book of organic baby purées

delicious home-cooked food for your baby

Topsy Fogg & Janice Fisher

Vermilion

Foreword

Topsy Fogg and Janice Fisher met, as pregnant mothers do, at National Childbirth Trust classes. Their babies, Maisie and Callum, were born one day apart in May 2000. During weaning, Topsy and Janice teamed up to share recipes using the best-quality organic ingredients. Other mums started asking for extra batches of their delicious baby food and they soon realised there was a demand for home-made-style baby food.

In 2001, Topsy and Janice launched Truuuly Scrumptious Organic Baby Food Ltd. Certified by the Soil Association, they are dedicated to

producing a range of delicious and nutritious food suitable from the first stages of weaning through to toddlers. The business started by supplying a few local shops; now they supply over 60 outlets as well as offering home delivery nation-wide. Since starting, they have won at least one food award a year for the quality and taste of their food.

Topsy and Janice's backgrounds have proved invaluable for starting the business and writing this book. Topsy, whose grandmother was a nanny and mother a maternity nurse, continued the family tradition and trained as a Norland Nanny. She has nannied for over 12 years during which time she weaned over 10 babies dealing with issues such as reflux, colic, food allergies and autism.

After school, Janice took a degree in Food Marketing Sciences, covering many aspects of food including nutrition and food hygiene. After graduating, she worked in the food industry for over 10 years before Truuuly Scrumptious began, developing new products and managing a portfolio of products for supermarkets. After the flurry of setting up the company, they have found time to each have a second child, Archie and Jack, who have been tasters for new recipes!

In this book Janice and Topsy share their delicious recipes, all tried-and-tested on their four children. They also set out the basic steps of weaning, baby nutrition and foundations of healthy eating in an easy to understand format.

contents

introduction

Just when you begin to get the hang of the breastfeeding or bottle routine, your baby will start waking again in the night and you are faced with the next hurdle: weaning! This important stage in your baby's development raises many questions and potential anxieties and, since the weaning guidelines changed to recommending that parents wait until six months rather than four months to introduce solids, we have received many questions from confused parents, from what age babies can start weaning to which foods can they have and when. We have also had many enquiries regarding food allergies. We hope to address these queries in our book, together with giving you some delicious recipe ideas, making the introduction to solids as worry-free and enjoyable as possible.

We cannot emphasise how important it is to give your baby the best start by choosing the right foods from the very beginning of their precious life. Thanks to food campaigners, like Lizzie Vann, who is continually funding research to identify the link between children's food and health, and Jamie Oliver, there is now a movement to remove the junk in our children's diet.

This is all great news but we need to start a lifetime of healthy eating right at the beginning. When we meet parents we ask if they would like to taste our baby food. The initial reaction is often, 'yuk, no thanks. I don't do baby food'. Why would you want to feed your little one food that you wouldn't even try yourself? We then persuade them to try a spoonful and they are amazed at just how delicious it is, and

it revolutionises their perception of baby food. This is how ALL baby food should be. Many people still have memories of reconstituted dried, canned or over-processed jars of food. They were tasteless, often with a gluey texture and managed to stain every bib – permanently!

By choosing good quality ingredients and following simple recipes, you will provide your baby with a wide range of flavours which will help them to grow to be less fussy eaters, who are willing to try new foods as they progress through childhood. The food that you choose for your baby will determine their growth and development and affect their immune system, which protects them against illness and keeps them healthy. At such a vulnerable stage when their immune system is not fully matured and they are growing rapidly, it is important to introduce a wide range of good quality foods which will include all the key nutrients.

In this book we have shared our favourite recipes. Some were created when we had our first children, Callum and Maisie, who were our inspiration to start the business. Others have been developed along the way and were trialled by our next two, Jack and Archie. We hope you enjoy making and eating them as much as we do – it's been difficult to stop the dads eating the extra portions which should have been frozen!

Although it is not always convenient to eat with your baby it is important to share some meals. As your baby develops he will notice if you are eating something different. Most of

Stage 2 recipes are suitable for all of the family to enjoy and it means you are all eating a healthy diet; just keep some aside before puréeing.

As your baby grows into a toddler you can involve him in decisions about what you are cooking, for example whether he would prefer spaghetti or pasta shapes with the pasta sauce.

We both cook many of our recipes regularly; Topsy cooks the Lamb and Apricot Casserole for supper with friends, accompanied with a lovely wholegrain mustard mash or couscous. I always seem to be cooking the Salmon and Broccoli Pie! I vary the type of fish used and add shell fish now the children are older; or rather than topping with mash I add pasta.

You may want to top up by buying from the Truuuly Scrumptious range of frozen organic ready-made meals, or you may find our No Added Salt Chicken or Vegetable Stock particularly useful, check out the website for details, www.bathorganicbabyfood.co.uk.

Babies and children are referred to throughout the book as 'he' for simplification. However, the information is equally applicable to both boys and girls unless otherwise specified.

introduction 7

part 1
the best possible start

healthy shopping

Before you begin to cook any kind of food for your baby, the most important thing to think about is how to source the best-quality ingredients for him. This means seeking out the finest fresh produce – preferably organic – at your local farm shop, farmers' market, deli or supermarket. Alternatively you can choose to have home delivery of a variety of foods from one of the many box schemes or organic delivery companies.

why organic?

Buying organic is sometimes regarded as a life-style choice and there is no doubt that it makes a difference to your weekly grocery bill. However, the health benefits for your growing baby, together with other environmental factors, are significant and we would urge you to try to use organic products when preparing the recipes in this book.

what does 'organic' mean?

Overall, organic farmers and organic food manu-facturers aim to produce food naturally, without the reliance on chemicals while protecting the environment. For example, farmers will use crop rotation to maintain soil fertility. They are bound by strict regulations and must be certified and inspected by an approved regulator, such as the Soil Association. In addition, they cannot use genetically modified (GM) crops.

Organic farmers are only permitted to use seven out of the hundreds of pesticides available. This encourages them to use natural preventa-tive methods against disease. Animals are reared without the use of drugs, antibiotics and wormers commonly used in intensive farming.

how do I know it's organic?

It is not enough for the food to be labelled as 'Organic', it must also have a symbol, and/or a code. The symbol means it complies with minimum government standards which meet European Union (EU) and international standards. Each European Union country has its own organic certification authority which conforms to EU and international standards.

Farmers wishing to move to an organic status must change their methods in line with organic regulations and then wait for a period of time (known as conversion) before they can claim to be organic. The farmer or food manufac-turer must decide which certification body to go with and then register, adhere to all the regulations and pass an inspection by their certification body. Thereafter they will be regularly inspected, including spot checks and unannounced visits. Food manufacturers are also only allowed to use permitted ingredients which meet the standards of the certification body.

why choose organic?

There are many reasons to choose organic alternatives for your shopping basket.

✿ **Improved animal welfare** – Organic regulations include rules regarding animal welfare. Improved welfare means the animals have a better environment to live in, which means they are better cared for physically and mentally. All organic animals must have access to the outdoors (weather permitting) and fewer animals must be kept (reduced stocking densities), which avoids intensive farming. More space per animal must be provided.

The table overleaf gives an example of the differences:

healthy shopping 11

chickens: what's the difference?

non-organic

A shed can house up to 250,000 birds

Birds are killed when they are 45 days old

Due to cramped conditions, birds are often aggressive and feather pecking is common so they are kept in semi-darkness to try and calm them. Clipping of beaks to reduce pecking is common.

70 per cent of all egg-laying chickens live in battery cages

Battery cages typically have the floor size of an A4 piece of paper

organic

The Soil Association sets a flock size of 500 or 1,000 where farmers can prove high levels of welfare

Birds are killed when they are 81 days old

The birds must spend two thirds of their life roaming outside

Minimum standard of 4 sq. m (5 sq. yd) for each bird, outside

Minimum standard of 10 birds per square metre in open sheds

✿ **Better diet for farm animals** – Animals bred for the organic market will have a more natural diet than non-organic and graze on pastures which have not been treated with artificial pesticides and fertilisers. Non-organic animals tend to have concentrated feedstuffs which can help increase yields. For example, organic dairy cattle produce one third less milk which reduces stress on the animal.

✿ **Better for the environment** – Organic farmers use crop rotation to maintain soil fertility. They do not use artificial fertilisers which get into streams and pollute the water, and they also use natural predators, such as beetles, spiders and birds, to control pests. The Soil Association monitors the effect on the environment and has found that there are 44 per cent more birds in fields on organic farms and five times as many wild plants. In addition, organic farming produces less carbon dioxide, the main

global warming gas. Farm workers are also less at risk to exposure to chemicals such as pesticides.

✿ **Restricted use of antibiotics** – During intensive farming most animals are fed antibiotics on a daily basis whether or not the animal is ill. As the bacteria which causes illness is exposed to these antibiotics daily, it can build up a resistance. It is possible for us to become ill from the same bacteria and then antibiotics may not be effective for us either. On organic farms animals are first treated with herbal or homeopathic remedies. They only receive antibiotics if these treatments are unsuccessful and if the animal is suffering. If an animal has been treated with antibiotics it must be withdrawn for a period. This period is three times longer for an organic animal compared to non-organic. As a result, organic animals tend to have stronger immunity to disease because they have been bred in better environments and have received a more natural diet.

the best possible start

what are the health benefits of choosing an organic diet?

There is a lack of evidence proving that organic food is more nutritious, however, it is widely accepted that organic milk contains almost two thirds more omega-3 fatty acids than non-organic milk. There are also recent studies which have found higher levels of vitamin C and antioxidants in organic fruit and vegetables.

However, concerns over pesticide residues in non-organic food highlight the benefits of choosing organic – pesticide residues are rarely found in organic food. Residues are commonly found in non-organic food and the government set maximum residue levels which are deemed to be safe. However, these maximum levels tend to be set for individual chemicals and there has been little research conducted on the 'cocktail effect' where a number of different chemical residues are present. Some research suggests that they may be hundreds of times more toxic than the same compounds individually.

In addition, food manufacturers producing organic food are not allowed to use many of the food additives which are thought to damage our health, such as hydrogenated fat, aspartame (artificial sweetener), monosodium glutamate (flavour enhancer) and artificial flavourings and colourings. Organic dried fruit is not allowed to use the preservative sulphur dioxide which is routinely used in non-organic dried fruits, even though it is known to provoke extreme allergic reactions in a small number of people, and can cause shortness of breath and aggravate digestive problems, such as Irritable Bowel Syndrome.

Organic food and farming prohibits the growing of any genetically modified (GM) crops and the use of any GM products, including feed for livestock. There are so many questions still not answered about the effect of GM foods and crops on humans and the environment, that many people choose to avoid them.

A long time before the BSE crisis, organic farming had not allowed the inclusion of animal protein in feedstuffs to farm animals. The Soil Association has found no recorded cases of BSE in any animal born and reared organically.

Why should I choose organic for my baby?

There are a large range of organic baby foods available; in fact over half of all baby food sold is organic. Because babies and children's body systems are not fully matured, they are not as good at dealing with toxins as adults are. A baby eats a greater weight of food to body weight compared to an adult and any pesticide residues will therefore have a greater effect.

The European Union has set pesticide residue limits for baby food, whether it's organic or not. This is monitored by random testing. By choosing organic you know that the farmers can only use seven of the hundreds of pesticides that are available, and the risk is minimised. As babies begin weaning with only fruit and vegetables, the risk of exposure to these residues is greater. Any toxins present in food are usually filtered out by our kidneys and excreted. However, babies' kidneys are not yet matured and will not be as efficient as an adults. Therefore if present, toxins will be harder to excrete and may remain in the body. GM crops are still under scrutiny – to avoid GM foods, choose organic.

healthy shopping 13

We would recommend that you buy organic or locally-produced, seasonal foods whenever possible. The range of organic foods available has increased dramatically over the last few years, with many supermarkets' own labels making it easier to choose the organic option, and this is especially true for baby and toddler food. Independent organic outlets are also becoming more widespread and there is a strong movement towards buying food produced locally to support the local economy as well as for environmental reasons. Here we have listed some of the options for buying organic and/or locally-produced foods (see also Useful Contacts, page 140).

❁ **Organic box schemes** – There are many companies which deliver organic produce to your door. A typical delivery contains a selection box of seasonal fruit and vegetables. Box schemes are usually operated by the grower or a group of farmers who have formed a group.

❁ **Organic delivery companies** – You can order specific types of food which can be delivered to your door, for example meats and cheeses. Some companies offer a wider range of organic products. They can deliver chilled and even frozen food which will arrive in insulated boxes.

❁ **Local farmers' markets** – Farmers' markets are growing rapidly. They are great for sourcing locally-produced food. You can often meet the farmers and producers themselves and even taste the product before you buy! Visit www.farmersmarkets.net for more information.

❁ **Farm shops** – Like farmers' markets, these are springing up all over the country. They may vary in size from a farm selling a few lines, such as eggs or cheese, to large farm shops selling wider ranges including meat.

❁ **Organic shops** – These are dedicated organic outlets selling a wide range of food, as well as non-food items such as organic cosmetics and clothing. They are listed in organic directories.

❁ **Delicatessens** – As well as selling the typical ranges of wines, olive oils and ingredients from around the world, they often stock organic and local produce.

❀ **Grow your own** – If you find the time you could always grow your own fruit and veg! Contact www.nsalg.org.uk (the National Society of Allotment and Leisure Gardeners) for a fact sheet on how to get started.

❀ **Supermarkets** – Some have dedicated organic sections, others stock organic products throughout the store. They tend to stock the larger organic brands and often have their own label alternative. Some supermarkets also stock local products.

organic vs. non-organic ingredients

Your organic or locally-produced shopping basket may differ in several ways to your regular, supermarket shop.

❀ **Appearance** – Fruit and vegetables in super-markets tend to be uniform in shape and with perfect skin. The supermarkets set standards for the growers who will use pesticides to ensure that the skin is blemish-free and regulated size. Organic and local produce is different. You may find vegetables are muddy and fruit is blemished, this is reassuring and shows that pesticides have been avoided. If you are using non-organic ingre-dients remember to peel produce; the skin is more likely to contain pesticide residues and is often waxed. Waxing helps preserve the fruit for longer but contains chemicals.

Organic meat and more premium meat may have a darker colour and a stronger smell. This is because it is often hung for longer before being minced or chopped. The extra hanging time helps improve the flavour as it allows it to develop.

Conversely, organic salmon tends to be paler in colour. Some non-organic salmon are fed food-stuffs which contain a colour that darkens the flesh of the fish.

❀ **Taste** – There have been some studies con-ducted to try and establish whether organic food tastes better or if people can taste the difference, but they all seem to reach different conclusions. We believe you can taste the difference. Vegetables and fruit tend to have more flavour. Some of the differences are also due to the way the ingredient been handled. Nothing beats trying it yourself!

❀ **Cost** – Organic food often costs more, but not always. Where it does cost more this reflects the different methods of production compared to non-organic farming. For example, yields are often lower – organic dairy cows produce typically one third less milk. Non-organic dairy cows receive feedstuffs which artificially increase their milk yield over and above what the cow would naturally produce.

why buy local?

- Reduces air miles
- Reduces packaging
- Supports local community and the rural economy
- Improves food knowledge, by meeting the producers and learning more about varieties of produce and breeds of animals.

seasonal choice

The development of the global market and improved distribution channels over recent decades have meant that seasonal fruit and vegetables are now available all year round – strawberries are on supermarket shelves in December and clementines in June. However, you will find that buying fruit and vegetables in their correct seasons has a number of benefits.

The produce will be fresher (it hasn't travelled so far); you are more likely to be buying UK-grown produce (unless it cannot be grown in the UK); and it is more economical – fruit and vegetables bought out of season can cost more. Use the table below to help you plan your recipes to include the freshest, healthiest ingredients (blue dots indicate the item is in season).

seasonal availability of UK crops

crop	Jan	Feb	Mar	Apr	May	Jun	Jul	Aug	Sept	Oct	Nov	Dec
beetroot						•	•	•	•	•		
broccoli						•	•	•	•	•	•	
brussel sprouts	•	•							•	•	•	•
cabbage (white)	•	•	•	•	•	•	•	•	•	•	•	•
carrots			•	•		•	•	•	•	•	•	•
cauliflower	•	•	•	•	•	•	•	•	•	•	•	•
courgette						•	•	•				
kale	•	•	•	•					•	•	•	•
leeks	•	•	•						•	•	•	•
parsnips	•	•							•	•	•	•
peas						•	•	•				
potato				•	•	•	•	•	•	•	•	•
pumpkin									•	•		
spinach					•	•	•	•	•	•		
squash (butternut)									•	•		
swede									•	•	•	
watercress								•	•	•		
apples	•	•	•					•	•	•	•	•
plums								•	•	•		
pears	•								•	•	•	•
raspberries						•	•	•	•			
strawberries					•	•	•	•				

essential nutrients

Now that you have filled your shopping basket with healthy, fresh produce it is important to understand how your baby can benefit from the essential nutrients that each food type has to offer. A well-balanced and varied diet is vital for your baby, ensuring good health and assisting your baby's development, along with training their taste buds to enjoy all the wonderful flavours and textures that you offer them.

nutrition for your baby

If you already follow a healthy diet, you may feel confident that you can follow similar guidelines for your baby. However, your baby's requirements for food are very different from your own. For example, current guidelines recommend that adults should reduce their fat intake but increase fibre. This is not the case for babies and toddlers, who require the calories to provide energy for rapid growth. Too much fibre for babies and toddlers will overload their underdeveloped digestive system and will reduce the absorption of vital minerals such as iron. Fibre can also make your baby feel full before their nutritional needs have been met. Babies who do not eat enough carbohydrates and fat will use protein for energy, instead of using it for essential growth and development.

The nutrients required for a growing child can be broken down into five main groups: protein, carbohydrate, fats, vitamins and minerals. Their benefits and sources are explained in detail below:

protein

Protein is required for healthy growth and development – every cell in your body requires protein for repair. As your baby is undergoing rapid growth and has an underdeveloped immune system, it is an essential nutrient. Foods containing protein should be fed to your baby after six months and only after you have introduced fruit and vegetables (see First Stage Recipes, pages 57–75). Introducing protein too early or feeding too much protein can strain your baby's immature kidneys. Overworking the kidneys will reduce their ability to remove waste from the body in the form of urine. In adults high-protein diets increase the risk of kidney stones. Protein consists of 22 amino acids; some of these cannot be made in the body and must be obtained in food. Meat, fish, soya and dairy products contain all these essential amino acids. And although other good sources of protein such as pulses and grains do not singularly contain all amino acids, by eating a wide variety or combining them, all the essential ones will be covered. This is particularly important for vegans.

Health benefits: Essential for growth, development and repair of tissues. Helps to provide good health and recovery.

Sources: Meat, such as beef, lamb, pork; poultry, such as chicken, turkey; fish, such as salmon, tuna; eggs; soya; quinoa; dairy products, especially cheese and milk; cereals; pulses, such as lentils, chickpeas; grains; nuts and seeds.

carbohydrate

Carbohydrate provides the body with energy (calories). Energy is required for the body to run its systems efficiently as well as for physical movement. When your baby is having three meals a day, about two thirds of your baby's diet should consist of carbohydrates.

There are two groups: refined and complex. Refined carbohydrates have had their natural fibre removed during processing. This natural fibre contains most of the valuable nutrients. As the natural fibre has been removed they are easy to digest and provide an instant source of energy. Food containing refined carbohydrates provides fewer nutrients and an immediate energy burst which, when gone, can leave you craving more. Complex carbohydrates retain their natural fibre and therefore keep all their valuable nutrients. They take longer to digest, releasing energy over a longer period of time. They are much better for your baby.

Health benefits: Provides energy which fuels growth and development.

Sources of refined carbohydrates: Sugar; biscuits; cakes; pastry; white bread; white flour.

Sources of complex carbohydrates: Porridge oats; wholemeal bread; rice; potatoes; wholemeal flour; wholegrain foods; pasta; avocado.

fat

Fat is a vital source of energy. It is also essential for surrounding and protecting our internal organs. It keeps our skin and arteries supple and is required for good brain functioning. A baby should not be on a low-fat diet, but should eat more of the 'right' kinds of fats. Fats can be divided into two main categories, saturated and unsaturated, which consists of two types – monounsaturated and polyunsaturated.

Health benefits: Source of energy, surrounds and protects internal organs. Omega-3 and omega-6 EFAs are vital for brain development (see page 20).

Saturated fats – These are derived mainly from animal sources. Babies should eat these foods in moderation. A diet rich in saturated fats causes increased deposits of fat in the arteries, eventually leading to heart disease in adults.

Sources: Meat; butter; hard cheese; coconut and palm oil.

Monounsaturated fats – These do not produce fatty deposits.

Sources: Certain types of oils, such as olive and rapeseed; avocado; nuts; seeds.

Polyunsaturated – These are the healthiest and include omega-3 and omega-6, which are essential fatty acids (EFAs). EFAs cannot be manufactured in the body and have to be sourced from foods. They are vital for brain development particularly in babies and children the immune system.

Sources: Oils, such as sunflower, cornflower, soya and fish oil; in particular omega-3 and omega-6 are found in fish oil, oily fish such as salmon, pilchards, sardines; nuts; seeds; tofu.

Trans fats or hydrogenated fats – oils which have been processed to form a solid or semi-solid, this is called 'hydrogenation'. This process damages the oils and destroys their nutritional value. They also have a negative effect on essential fatty acids. A lot of food manufacturers and supermarkets have stopped using them. Check the label to be sure they are not present.

Sources: Processed food such as margarine; biscuits; crisps; pastries and pies.

brain food

It is the long chain polyunsaturated fatty acids, such as omega-3 and omega-6, which are particularly important for brain development and development of the nervous system of the foetus. Omega-3s are essential fatty acids (EFAs) which cannot be made in the body and must be consumed in the diet. They also keep cholesterol levels low, protecting the heart. Omega-3s are therefore extremely important for the expectant mother, babies and children. The benefits of omega-3s have been well published, most notably in the Durham Schools Trial in 2004 which proved that children taking an omega-3 supplement made dramatic improvements in reading and spelling.

Sources of omega-3s: Oily fish is recognised as a good source of omega-3. However, the average intake of oily fish for adults is very low. In fact seven out of ten people never eat oily fish at all. Although many people will eat salmon, sardines, pilchards and mackerel are less popular. Omega-3s are present in other foods, but at lower levels. The table opposite provides a comparison.

sources of omega-3

food (100g)	grams of omega-3
fish	
Salmon	2.3g
Sardines	2.2g
Pilchards	2.2g
Mackerel	2.0g
Tuna	1.6g
Trout	1.2g
other sources	
Walnuts*	10.4g
Pumpkin seeds*	8.0g
1 tbsp flaxseed oil	6.9g
Soya beans	1.0g
Sesame seeds*	0.4g
Poppy seeds*	0.4g
Tofu	0.3g
Pumpkin/Butternut squash	0.3g
Brussel sprouts	0.3g
Broccoli	0.2g
Cauliflower	0.2g

See advice on nuts for babies on page 37.

vital vitamins

Vitamins and minerals provide a crucial role in maintaining a healthy body. They are also required for key functions, such as preventing anaemia. Our bodies are unable to make most vitamins and minerals, so they must be obtained from a varied healthy diet.

vitamins

Vitamins can be divided into two groups: water-soluble and fat-soluble.

❀ **Water-soluble** – Vitamins C and the Bs are water-soluble. Apart from vitamin B12, they cannot be stored in the body, and therefore cannot be overdosed. As a result they need to be eaten regularly. As the name suggests, these vitamins can be dissolved in water and during cooking some of the vitamin content can be lost through evaporation.

❀ To maximise vitamin retention, try not to overcook food and, where possible, use cooking methods such as steaming, rather than boiling.

❀ During storage, fruit and vegetables start to lose small amounts of water-soluble vitamins, so consume fruit and vegetables as soon as you can after purchase.

❀ For really fresh produce, shop at farm shops which stock local produce stored for a shorter period of time than many of their supermarket equivalents.

❀ **Fat-soluble** – Vitamins A, D, E and K are found in fatty foods. They are absorbed by the body into the circulation which carries them to the liver where they are stored, apart from vitamin E which is distributed throughout the body's fatty tissues. The vitamins are then released by the body as they are required. A build-up of these vitamins leading to an excess can be harmful.

minerals

Small amounts of minerals are essential in our diet in order for the body to work properly. They are required for many different functions.

reusing the cooking water or juices in a meal will put some of the vitamins back

vitamin and mineral fact file

vitamin	function	source
A (retinol) Fat-soluble	Essential to maintain healthy skin, promote healthy growth, for normal vision and for the immune system. Found as retinol in foods from animal sources or as carotenoids in foods from plant sources. Betacarotene, the pigment that gives the green, yellow and orange colour to vegetables and fruit, is the most common carotenoid and is an antioxidant.	liver; eggs; full-fat dairy products; oily fish; carrots; spinach; red peppers; mangoes; apricots
B complex *(includes B1, B2, B3, B5, B6, B12, folic acid and biotin)* Water-soluble	Most B vitamins are involved in assisting the digestion of food in order to produce energy, assisting in the maintenance of the immune system and the nervous system. B complex vitamins are particularly important for growing babies as they help make energy available to fuel the growing process	wholemeal bread; breakfast cereals; dairy produce, especially eggs and cheese; green leafy vegetables; liver; oily fish, such as sardines, pilchards; yeast extract
C (ascorbic acid) Water-soluble	Essential for the growth and repair of body tissues, healthy gums, healing wounds and for providing a good immune system. Antioxidant (see page 24). Enables the body to absorb non-haem iron (see page 26) found in bread and cereals.	green leafy vegetables, such as curly kale and broccoli; peppers; brussel sprouts; fruits including berries, particularly blueberries, blackcurrants, kiwi fruit, mangoes and citrus fruits
D Fat-soluble	We get most of our vitamin D from exposure to sunlight. Normal exposure is enough to generate the vitamin which is made by our skin. The vitamin then travels to the liver where it is stored. It is important for babies and children to eat foods rich in vitamin D as the use of sun screen will potentially reduce the ability of the skin to manufacture its own vitamin D	eggs; oily fish, such as sardines and pilchards; dairy products

vitamin	function	source
E Fat-soluble	Helps protect the tissues in the body. Antioxidant. It helps protect against heart disease and maintains a healthy nervous system	sweet potatoes; avocados, wholemeal bread; seeds
K Fat-soluble	Essential for allowing wounds to heal properly as it helps the blood to clot. Helps to build strong bones. Found in many foods and can also be made in the body by bacteria in the gut. Because it is present in a number of foods, deficiency is rare.	green leafy vegetables, such as broccoli and spinach; small amounts in meat and dairy products

mineral		
Calcium	Most important for the development of strong bones and teeth. Essential for nerve and muscle function and is also involved in blood clotting. Vitamin D is required for the body to absorb calcium. When a baby's milk intake is reduced as weaning progresses it is important to intro- duce foods rich in calcium.	most easily absorbed from dairy products, such as milk and cheese; tinned sardines and pilchards; broccoli; curly kale; almonds (see advice on nuts for babies, page 37)
Iron	A baby is born with a store of iron which lasts about six months. After that time foods providing a good source of iron should be included in the baby's diet during weaning. Premature babies may not have developed their six month's store. Contact your doctor or health visitor for advice. Iron is essential for the formation of haemoglobin in red blood cells which transports oxygen around the body. Oxygen is required all over the body to make energy available, so there is a constant need for haemoglobin.	bread and many breakfast cereals are fortified with iron; liver and red meats; eggs (mainly the yolk); oily fish, such as sar- dines and pilchards; green leafy vegetables, such as broccoli and spinach; dried apricots; pulses
Zinc	Essential for growth and a healthy immune system. Deficiency is rare.	red meat; dairy prod- ucts; eggs; fish; whole- grain cereals; pulses

The term 'superfoods' has been given to a range of fruit and vegetables that contain 'phytonutrients'. These recently discovered compounds provide health benefits over and above the basic nutritional minerals and vitamins. Over a hundred phytonutrients have been found in plant foods and are responsible for giving plants their colour, flavour and smell.

They can provide us with many health benefits including healing and helping to prevent illnesses such as cancer and heart disease. Phytonutrients often act as antioxidants, counteracting the damaging effects of free radicals. As cells in your body carry out their normal functions they naturally produce toxic molecules called 'free radicals' which cause damage to other cells. Antioxidants that naturally occur in the body or those obtained from foods can prevent this damage by neutralising their harmful effects. Free radicals have been linked with heart disease, cancer and other age-related diseases. Many fruits and vegetables contain antioxidants.

There are many variations on the list of 'superfoods'. The table opposite shows ours, which is not just appropriate for babies and toddlers, but for all the family.

Quinoa – Although not officially a super-food, this grain contains more protein than any other. Quinoa (pronounced keen-wah) is a small seed which, when cooked, has a fine texture similar to couscous. The protein is of an unusu-ally high quality containing all the amino acids (most grains lack one or two amino acids). It is therefore an excellent food for vegetarians and vegans. It is easy to digest and fairly bland so can be added to sweet or savoury dishes and is a great basis for a meal for growing babies.

the best possible start

lovely superfoods for lively families

superfood	nutrients	benefits
Avocado	Nutrient dense food, with vitamins E (antioxidant) and B6 minerals, particularly potassium. Also contains protein and monounsaturated fat.	Vitamin B6 and potassium are important for a healthy nervous system. Potassium also helps reduce blood pressure.
Bananas	Good source of carbohydrate. Rich in potassium.	Carbohydrate provides a healthy energy burst. Potassium is important for a healthy nervous system and helps to reduce blood pressure.
Berries (such as blueberries, strawberries etc)	Vitamin C and other antioxidants. Soluble fibre.	Blueberries contain large amounts of antioxidants. The fibre helps maintain a healthy digestive tract.
Broccoli	Excellent source of vitamin C and many phytonutrients. Contains folic acid.	Thought to help in the fight against heart disease and some cancers. Folic acid is essential for a healthy nervous system and helps the body release energy from food.
Kiwi fruit	Rich source of vitamin C which acts as an antioxidant. Also contains potassium and a phytonutrient called lutein.	Vitamin C counteracts damaging free radicals and helps in healing. Potassium for a healthy nervous system. Lutein helps maintain healthy eyesight.
Oily fish, such as salmon, pilchards and sardines	Rich in omega-3 fats. Also contain selenium and vitamin E.	Omega-3 fats are vital for brain development. Selenium protects against heart disease. Vitamin E also helps fight heart disease and maintains a healthy nervous system.
Orange vegetables, such as carrots, sweet potatoes etc	Rich in betacarotene, an antioxidant. Contain vitamins C and E, also antioxidants.	Antioxidants help with the fight against some cancer and heart disease.
Tomatoes	Contain the phytonutrient lycopene. Also rich in vitamin C.	Lycopene gives tomatoes their red colour. It helps fight against cancer and heart disease. Vitamin C counteracts damaging free radicals and helps in healing.

the vegetarian baby

We meet many parents wishing to wean their babies on a vegetarian or vegan diet. This is a perfectly healthy option, however, more care is required in order to provide all the vital nutrients in their diet. This is especially important for babies on a vegan diet, which is at risk of being deficient in calcium, iron, zinc, vitamin B12, vitamin D, vitamin B2 and protein. We would advise you to contact your health visitor for guidance.

Providing a varied vegetarian diet is the key to supplying all nutrients.

✿ **Iron** – Babies are born with their own store of iron but this will be depleted by the age of six months. Iron is less easily absorbed from non-animal sources (non-haem iron), but its absorption can be improved by the inclusion of vitamin C in the meal. High-fibre foods will also reduce iron absorption so avoid high-fibre cereals. Include fresh fruit or vegetables in the meal to provide vitamin C.

Sources: Apricots; refined lentils; cereals; beans such as butter beans; green vegetables.

✿ **Zinc** – Essential for growth and a healthy immune system.

Sources: Seeds; ground nuts; whole grains; pulses.

✿ **Calcium** – Breast or formula milk contains all the calcium your baby needs initially. In the later weaning stages provide extra calcium in your baby's food.

Sources: Cow's and fortified soya milk; soya yogurts; cheese; green vegetables; wholemeal bread; beans, pulses, lentils; ground almonds; sesame paste; tofu.

✿ **Protein** – Required for healthy growth and development and cell repair. Protein is made up of amino acids, of which there are 22 in total. Some amino acids cannot be made in the body so must be provided through dietary sources. Meat, fish, soya, quinoa and dairy products contain all of these 22 amino acids. Pulses, such as lentils and beans, provide some but not all 22 amino acids. They must be eaten in variety or combination in order to provide the full complement.

Sources: Pulses such as lentils; tofu; beans; dairy product; eggs.

✿ **Energy** (Carbohydrates) – Babies need energy to fuel growth and to allow the body to function properly. Processed foods high in sugar and refined carbohydrates, such as cakes and biscuits, will provide an unhealthy energy burst which will disappear quickly. They are also bad for your baby's gums and teeth. It is much better to provide complex carbohydrates which release energy slowly.

Sources: Pasta; oats; rice; potatoes; avocado; sesame seed spread.

✿ **Vitamin B12** – Vegetarian babies should obtain enough of this vitamin from dairy products and eggs. Vegan babies will need vitamin B12 from fortified foods such as margarine, some soya milks, low-salt yeast extract and breakfast cereals.

✿ **Vitamin B2** – Good sources include low salt yeast extract, mushrooms and fortified breakfast cereals.

✿ **Vitamin D** – Made by the body when skin is exposed to sunlight. Vegetarian babies will get their vitamin D from dairy products such as eggs and yoghurts. Vegan babies may need vitamin D supplements – talk to your health visitor or doctor.

✿ **Fibre** – Babies do not require a high-fibre diet as it reduces the absorption of essential nutrients, such as iron, zinc and calcium.

✿ **Essential Fatty Acids** (EFAs) – Found in plant-based sources, although they are not quite the same as those present in fish oils.

Sources: Oils, such as linseed, flaxseed, walnut and rapeseed; sesame seed spread; ground nuts and seeds.

✿ **Quorn and textured vegetable protein** – Tofu (soya bean curd) is recognised as an ideal food for babies. It is an excellent source of protein and easily digested. Quorn products are perfectly safe for children and babies but they are lower in calories and have a higher fibre content than meat so should be used sparingly. Always check the salt content of foods (see page 37).

eating a variety of fruit and vegetables will provide a good range of vitamins and minerals as well as a variety of phytonutrients

feeding your baby

Weaning is the process of introducing solid foods into your baby's diet in order to fulfill their growing nutritional needs. This is a new stage and will be a journey of discovery. Babies' reactions to the first stages of weaning vary. Callum looked at the spoon bemused while Jack took his first few spoonfuls and seemed to be saying 'why didn't you give me this before'! Some babies wait open-mouthed in anticipation for the next spoonful while others will need encouragement, particularly when trying new flavours.

It is now believed that exposing babies to foods too early may increase the likelihood of the baby suffering from a food allergy. Before 17 weeks, a baby's intestine is immature and porous. Introducing food at this stage will mean the food passes through the intestine and into the bloodstream, where the immune system identifies foreign material and initiates an attack. Although you would not see an allergic reaction on the first occasion, the body remembers the foreign material so the next time the food is consumed it may trigger an allergic reaction. This is why the World Health Organization (WHO) and the UK Department of Health have revised their recommendations.

The WHO recommends exclusive breastfeeding for the first six months 'to achieve optimal growth, development and health'. However, in the UK the Department of Health recognises that although exclusive breastfeeding for six months is nutritionally adequate, there should be some flexibility in this advice as all babies –breast- or bottle-fed – develop at different rates. They recommend that babies are NOT weaned BEFORE 17 weeks.

It is particularly important to wait until six months before weaning if you have a family history of allergies, as the incidence of adverse reactions, allergies and coeliac disease does decrease if you delay weaning until this time.

too early

You should not wean your baby before 17 weeks because:

✿ They cannot make all the right enzymes they need to digest food.

✿ They have immature kidneys.

✿ They have poor head control and cannot maintain the correct position for swallowing.

✿ Their digestive system could be damaged and gastroenteritis will be more common.

✿ There is more risk of developing allergies, including eczema and asthma.

too late

Most babies are ready to wean at six months because:

✿ Babies are born with only sufficient iron reserves for the first six months. After this it is essential that he obtains iron from his diet (iron is an important factor in brain development. Iron deficiency early on in life may have a profound influence on learning development).

✿ Jaw and tongue have developed to cope with eating and swallowing foods.

✿ Learning to deal with foods helps a baby's mouth and tongue develop and prepare for speech.

✿ Up to the age of six months of age babies learn to accept new tastes, flavours and textures – if you leave it too late there may be less time for him to acquire good eating habits.

When you see the signs that your baby is ready you can begin giving him his first tastes of food. These tastes are more of a learning experience and shouldn't replace any milk feeds. Breast milk or formula will still be your baby's main source of nutrition.

Your baby will let you know when he is ready for food when:

✿ He can hold his head up and control his head movements.

✿ He sits well when supported.

✿ He is still hungry after a milk feed.

✿ He demands feeds more frequently.

✿ He wakes at night with hunger after having previously slept through the night.

✿ He attempts to put things in his mouth.

✿ He makes chewing motions.

✿ His weight gain slows or levels out without a period of illness to explain why.

✿ He shows interest in what you're eating.

get ready!

Choose a time which is convenient for you and when you are both relaxed. A good time to try is towards the end of a lunchtime or afternoon milk feed. Ensure your baby is not too hungry or too tired as he may be more likely to be disinterested or frustrated and not enjoy this new experience.

✿ Be prepared – have bibs, a cloth or wipes and a change of clothes to hand, and possibly something on the floor. It can be a messy experience!

✿ Make sure he is comfortable – use a high chair if he can sit well, otherwise a bouncing chair or sit him supported in your arms.

do not wean
babies before
the age of 17 weeks

the best possible start

go! tips & techniques for feeding

After your baby has his usual breast milk or formula, when he is nearly satisfied, give him one or two teaspoons of iron-enriched organic baby rice on a soft rubber-tipped spoon mixed with breast milk or formula to the consistency of thin soup. Then finish the remaining milk feed. Introducing new food at this time during a feed will help ensure that he isn't too hungry to become frustrated at trying the new food and not too full to be disinterested.

✿ The baby rice should be lukewarm or at room temperature. Your baby is more likely to accept the food if it as at a similar temperature to the milk he has been having.

✿ Place the spoon gently into your baby's mouth. He may start to suck the food but if he is unsure you can tip the spoon up slightly so that the mixture gently slides into his mouth then remove it so that he can attempt to swallow. Never force the spoon into his mouth.

Some babies may push out the first food offered to them with their tongue for the first couple of times. This is because they are used to pushing their tongue against the nipple or teat to get milk. Don't worry and continue to offer them food as they will learn to take food to the back of their mouth and swallow. Be patient; it may take time to learn these new skills!

If your baby is reluctant to start with spoon-feeding you can always offer a small amount of food on your clean finger and let your baby suck it off and try again in a day or two with a spoon.

When your baby is taking about three teaspoons of baby rice and eating well with a spoon you can introduce other foods.

recipe for success

✿ Go at your baby's pace. Allow plenty of time when you first start. Remember your baby needs to move food to the back of his tongue and then swallow. The food is going to taste and feel different and he will need to learn that food doesn't come in a continuous flow.

✿ Start with bland foods which are easy to digest and unlikely to provoke an allergic reaction. Make them almost as liquid as milk, organic baby rice is perfect – we recommend Organix First Organic Baby Rice, which is widely available.

✿ Give your baby one new taste at a time – that way you will know better which they prefer and detect any adverse reactions.

✿ Don't force food on your baby; let your baby tell you how much they want; it is quite normal for him to consume four or five teaspoons at one feed and very little the next.

feeding your baby

stage 1 17 weeks

The first stage of weaning takes your baby from simple spoonfuls of plain baby rice to first tastes of smooth purées of fruit and vegetables. You can begin at 17 weeks if your baby appears ready (see page 29) or start at the recommended six months. This stage lasts for approximately two to four weeks depending when you started weaning; then your baby should be ready to move on to the second stage, as long as he has reached six months.

If you feel that your baby is ready to wean before six months speak to your health visitor, dietitian or nutritionist first. If you do wean before six months, you will need to avoid the following foods, which can be introduced only after six months:

Foods to avoid before six months:

❀ Gluten, such as wheat, rye, barley, oats, bread, pasta, flour, breakfast cereals, rusks.

❀ Eggs.

❀ Dairy products, such as cow's milk, cheese, yoghurt, fromage frais, custard.

❀ Fish and shellfish (introduce shellfish after 12 months).

❀ Citrus fruit (including orange juice).

first tastes

Once your baby has taken baby rice for about three to five days you can progress to the next stage and start to introduce other tastes in simple vegetable and fruit purées (see Meal Planner, page 55).

If you started weaning before six months, this next stage will be a more gradual progression over the course of about three to four weeks. If you started at six months, this next stage will be much shorter, about two weeks.

When babies reach six months their iron stores are depleted and they cannot get enough from milk. Therefore if you start weaning at six months, it is important to include vegetable and fruit purées that contain iron. Foods rich in vitamin C will help the absorption of iron as well.

Suitable first foods

❀ Baby rice.

❀ Vegetable purées (carrot, squash, sweet potato, swede, parsnip).

❀ Fruit purées (apple, banana, pear).

We recommend starting with a vegetable purée. This can either be on its own or mixed with a little baby rice and breast or formula milk. Fruit can be introduced after your baby has had a few different vegetables, to avoid the development of a sweet tooth. For the same reason, there is no need to mix fruit with a vegetable purée in

 the best possible start

a meal. The vegetables listed above have a naturally sweet taste that your baby will enjoy.

It is advisable to offer the same new food for a couple of days so your baby gets used to the new tastes and textures and so you can watch out for any signs of a possible allergic reaction such as diarrhoea, tummy aches or rashes.

Once your baby has become used to the tastes of different foods you can start to combine previously tried vegetables for variety. If you baby rejects any new food, try it again a few days later or combine it with another purée or baby rice.

You can gradually increase the amount of food you give to your baby and start to introduce food earlier on in the feed. You will also need to gradually move from giving food once a day to twice, then eventually three times a day.

when serving your baby's food, ensure it has been thoroughly heated, then leave to cool; it should be warm, similar to body temperature – stir it thoroughly and check the temperature

stage 2 6 – 12 months

Now that your baby is enjoying a range of interesting flavours, colours and textures of food, you can extend his repertoire even further with the introduction of dairy products, gluten and protein, such as meat, fish and pulses. This exciting stage should be taken slowly, with the gradual introduction of thicker texture and more sophisticated flavours.

Milk is still an important part of your baby's diet and until 12 months your baby will need up to 500–600 ml (1 pt) per day. During this second stage of weaning you can make your baby's purées coarser to encourage him to chew. Start to leave small soft lumps in the semi-purée. If the lumps have to be chewed they are too hard. Soft lumps will be ground down by gums or teeth, if he has any.

And remember, never leave your baby unattended while eating because of the risk of choking.

new foods

Once weaning has been established you can include second stage recipes that start to introduce a greater range of flavours, and essential nutrients, into your growing baby's diet.

Protein

✿ Include protein every day.

✿ If you are introducing meat into your baby's diet it is best to start with a little puréed chicken mixed with vegetables, as it is easier for your baby to digest. You can then progress on to red meats.

✿ Try fish like cod, salmon, tuna or trout, either fresh or canned. If you buy the canned varieties choose ones in water or oil, and avoid those in brine which will have a high salt content. Avoid smoked fish as it is usually cured in salt before the smoking process and can often contain additives and dyes.

✿ Eggs can be introduced in small amounts but must be well cooked. Some babies are allergic to eggs so watch for any reactions.

✿ Quinoa, pulses (beans and lentils), soya-based foods (tofu) are also good non-meat sources of protein.

Dairy products

✿ You should always give full-fat dairy products to your baby, as they need it for growth and development.

✿ You can buy yoghurts or fromage frais for younger babies which tend to use fruit purées to sweeten rather than sugar. Check the labels. Alternatively, buy natural yoghurt and sweeten it with a home-made fruit purée.

✿ Use hard pasteurised cheeses such as Cheddar, Edam or Gruyère. Avoid unpasteurised and blue cheese like Stilton, or soft cheeses, such as Brie or Camembert as they may contain *Listeria* which is a food-poisoning bacteria.

✿ You can use soft processed cheese, like Philadelphia cream cheese or ricotta.

✿ You can use cow's milk in your baby's cooking, for example when making a cheese sauce, but you cannot give it to your baby as a drink until he is 12 months, as it does not provide the correct balance of nutrients. You should offer full-fat milk to your child from 12 months to 2 years, as he still needs the fat and vitamins that the full-fat variety provides.

Gluten

✿ Foods containing gluten, such as pasta, bread and flour, are an excellent source of energy, vitamins, minerals and fibre.

✿ Once you have established weaning, two to three servings of these foods are recommended daily.

Iron

✿ It is important to add foods which are rich in iron into your baby's diet. Vitamin C helps with the absorption of iron – include foods rich in vitamin C at the same time.

your older baby's needs

Once your baby is on the move you will probably need to increase the amount of food given and gradually reduce the amount of milk offered until you drop a milk feed (lunch time is usually a good feed to do this).

You will still need to offer a drink. We recommend you offer your baby cooled boiled water in a beaker or cup; avoid mineral water as some have mineral contents which are unsuitable for babies. You can offer fresh diluted one part fruit juice to 10 parts cooled boiled water. It is better to offer this in a beaker or cup rather than a bottle to reduce the potential damage to your baby's teeth from the sugar.

At this point of weaning, where possible, you should be eating with your baby. Your baby is constantly learning and absorbing information. By eating with your baby you will be teaching him that eating is a pleasurable and sociable experience. Our recipes are just as delicious for older siblings and adults, so you can all share a meal together.

During the second stage of weaning, you should start to introduce finger foods to encourage your baby to feed himself and chew, even if he has no teeth.

Suitable finger foods:

✿ Toast/pitta bread 'fingers'

✿ Peeled apple

✿ Banana

✿ Home-made rusks

✿ Cooked and cooled carrot sticks, broccoli, green beans

Teething

Babies can cut their first teeth anytime in the first year but most often around six months. Teething can be painful and it may make your baby irritable and fractious. Symptoms include one red cheek, excessive dribbling, runny nose and sometimes a bout of diarrhoea. He may like to bite on hard objects to try and alleviate his painful gums. During teething it may make your baby fussy about what he eats.

If he has mastered finger foods, you could offer cooked and chilled vegetables like carrot sticks, to help soothe his gums.

stage 3 12 months

Your baby will now have progressed to three meals a day and possibly two snacks between meals. Those snacks can include fresh fruit, rice cakes or home-made rusks. Avoid sweet biscuits or sugary rusks so your baby doesn't get into the habit of expecting something sweet. Fruit will be satisfying while providing the correct nutrients.

Your baby's food should now be chopped rather than puréed and your baby will probably be trying to feed himself; if not he should be encouraged at this stage.

Make sure that your baby has a varied diet to ensure all of his nutritional needs are met. His diet should consist of food from all of the food groups listed in the table below.

If your baby is vegetarian you must ensure you offer two servings a day of pulses, lentils/split peas and tofu or soya pieces to enable him to get all the energy and nutrients he needs. You will also need to include plenty of fruit and vegetables which contain vitamin C; this will help with the absorption of iron (see page 23).

foods to avoid

What you choose to feed your baby in these early months will get them off to the best possible start. Making the right choices and avoiding unhealthy foods will set the foundations for good health and good eating habits.

a balanced diet

food groups	what it is good for?
Milk and dairy products, e.g. cheese, yoghurt, fromage frais	Strong healthy bones and teeth
Carbohydrates, e.g. bread, pasta, rice and cereals	Provides energy
Fruit and vegetables	Builds natural immunity and promotes general healthy growth and development
Protein, e.g. meat, fish, eggs, beans and pulses	Strong muscles and bones. Brain and eye development

the best possible start

Salt

❀ Never add salt to your baby's food because his kidneys have not matured enough to cope with it

❀ Babies up to six months old should have less than 1g of salt a day. From seven months to a year they should have a maximum of 1g of salt a day. Babies will be getting a sufficient level of salt through breast or formula milk.

❀ If you are cooking for the whole family take out your baby's portion before adding salt to the remainder, or leave salt out altogether.

❀ Flavours can be developed in other ways, such as with the addition of herbs and or no added salt stock (see page 51).

❀ Remember that some foods can contain high levels of salt, for example cheese, bacon and sausages, so limit the amount given. Processed foods, like pasta sauces, breakfast cereals, stocks and yeast-based spreads, can contain high levels of salt and must be avoided. It is important to be aware of salt levels as your baby grows:

1–3 years	→	2g a day (0.8g sodium)
4–6 years	→	3g a day (1.2g sodium)
7–10 years	→	5g a day (2g sodium)
11 and over	→	6g a day (2.5g sodium)

(Food Standards Agency Guidelines)

These are *maximums*; it is better to have less than this.

Sugar

❀ Avoid adding sugar to any food you give your baby, it will encourage a sweet tooth and will lead to tooth decay when the milk teeth start to come through.

❀ Excessive sugar is converted to energy very quickly, creating a quick, unnatural energy burst which leaves him feeling low and craving more sugar.

Honey

❀ Honey is not recommended for babies under a year. Very occasionally it can contain bacteria which will produce toxins in your baby's intestine and can cause a serious illness called infant botulism. When your baby is a year old his intestine has matured and the bacteria is unable to grow.

Whole nuts

❀ Whole nuts are not recommended for children under five years as they are a choking hazard.

❀ As long as there is no family history of allergies, particularly hay fever, asthma or eczema, babies over six months are able to have flaked or crushed nuts (peanut butter) and seeds.

❀ If the baby's parents, brothers or sisters have a food allergy or other allergic conditions, such as hay fever, asthma and/or eczema, then the baby will have a higher risk of developing a peanut allergy.

❀ Peanut allergies affect 1 per cent of people and can cause severe reactions. If you fall within this category, to reduce the risk avoid eating peanuts and peanut products while you are breastfeeding and during weaning. Wait until your child is three years old before introducing peanut or peanut products. If you think your child might be allergic to peanuts, speak to your doctor.

Adult foods

❀ Processed foods need to be avoided as they often contain high levels of sugars and salts.

❀ Check the labels as they may also contain unwanted additives, preservatives and thickeners.

❀ Tea and coffee should be avoided as they contain tannins, which inhibit the absorption of iron. They also contain caffeine.

❀ Fizzy drinks should be avoided as they will have a high sugar content which will lead to tooth decay. They will also curb the appetite which will lead to poor weight gain. The low-sugar alternatives are no better as they contain artificial sweeteners (aspartame, saccharin) and will still encourage a sweet tooth and can cause an upset stomach.

❀ Low-fat dairy products are not suitable for children under two as fat is an important source of calories, vitamins and minerals that are essential for your baby's growth and development.

Raw eggs

❀ Foods containing raw or partially-cooked eggs should be avoided due to the risk of salmonella poisoning.

Soft cheese

❀ Processed soft cheese is safe to give your baby. Cheeses such as Brie and Camembert should not be used as they may contain the food-poisoning bacteria *Listeria* which babies are more sensitive to.

Shellfish

❀ Avoid giving your baby shellfish until he is 12 months. Shellfish can cause an allergic reaction and also have a higher risk of causing food poisoning.

Stock cubes

❀ Many recipes, including ours, suggest you use vegetable or meat stocks in the baby purées. Do NOT use regular stock cubes. Stock cubes contain high levels of salt and are NOT suitable for babies or children.

❀ You can either make the stock at home (see page 51) or you can substitute with the cooking water from cooked vegetables.

❀ Alternatively, use our Truuuly Scrumptious No Added Salt Frozen Organic Chicken and Vegetable Stock. See www.bathorganicbabyfood.co.uk for the list of stockists and home delivery.

buying ready-made baby food

Sometimes it's just not possible or practical to make all of your baby's food at home, especially if you're out for the day or on holiday. There are many types of ready-made baby food available in jars, cans, pouches, fresh and frozen. If you are planning to buy ready-made food, look for organic labels and shop wisely:

the best possible start

✿ **Watch out for very sweet-tasting savoury products** – Some brands are very misleading and sell what you believe is a savoury dish but actually contains a high percentage of fruit (between 40 and 70 per cent). This fruit sweetens the food and makes it more appealing to your baby. Fruit will not always be mentioned in the name of the product but when you check the list of ingredients you find it is actually the main ingredient! Check the ingredients list on the back of the pack – they will be listed in descending order of weight. If your baby is eating a lot of savoury food which is sweetened with fruit, it will encourage a sweet tooth.

✿ **Purées** – Unfortunately the majority of commercial baby food is sold as complete purées and there is no gradual increase to lumps, even in food for older babies. This encourages your baby to expect purées and reject lumps. Look for brands which increase texture for older babies.

✿ **No added sugar** – Check the label; some products have added sugar.

✿ **Hidden sugar** – Check the label, other words for sugar include: molasses, dextrose, sucrose and glucose.

✿ **No added salt** – Check no salt has been added; and check the overall salt level is low. Sometimes ingredients containing high levels of salt have been used which results in a high salt level even though salt was not added as a separate ingredient. Some foods only label salt as 'sodium', (see page 37 to check the salt equivalent).

✿ **Additives** – Choose brands with no artificial colourings and flavourings, bulking agents or artificial sweeteners, such as aspartame.

✿ **Before six months** – Unfortunately some manufacturers choose to ignore the guidelines and include ingredients unsuitable for babies less than six months old, for example pasta which contains gluten.

frequently asked questions

what age can I start weaning?
In the UK, the Department of Health recommends that babies are NOT weaned BEFORE 17 weeks. Most health visitors will advise you to wait until six months, but speak to them if you feel that your baby is ready to wean before then (see also page 29).

how long should my baby be eating fruit and vegetable purées before I can introduce stage 2 foods, such as meat?
Your baby should have reached six months of age and been eating fruit and vegetable purées for three to four weeks prior to introducing Stage 2 foods. If you started weaning at six months, the first stage of weaning with fruit and vegetable purées will be much shorter, about two weeks.

why won't my baby eat thicker purées and why does he spit out the lumps?
There could be several explanations:

✿ **Spent too long on smooth purées** – When weaning, don't be afraid to introduce some texture quite soon. If you stay too long on smooth purées, then that is what he will expect in the future. As the majority of commercial baby food is completely puréed, you'll need to pay close attention to find brands which increase texture for older babies. If you are making your own food, introduce soft lumps as soon as possible.

✿ **Hard lumps** – When you start to introduce texture you need to purée for less time, leaving soft lumps. If the lumps are too hard and would need to be chewed, for example tiny lumps of slightly undercooked carrot, they will be rejected. Even if your baby has no teeth he will grind soft lumps with his gums.

✿ **Keep trying** – If your baby keeps rejecting the lumps, purée slightly more until you reach an acceptable texture. You may have to introduce texture very slowly.

✿ **Try more texture on their favourite meal** – When you start to introduce some texture use your baby's favourite recipes. They are more likely to accept lumps with a taste they are comfortable with, rather than trialling a new recipe at the same time. It is worth persevering with the lumpier foods as it is important that he learns to chew and this will help with speech development.

how much food should my baby be eating?
There are no hard and fast rules. It will depend on many factors, such as their original birth weight, whether they are breast- or formula-fed, how active they are... But as a guide, by the time

your baby is eight months old he should be eating three solid meals a day, making sure you are giving a variety of protein, carbohydrates, fruit and vegetables as well as 500–600 ml (1 pt) of breast or formula milk.

I need to reduce my baby's milk feeds, which one should I drop first?

As your baby increases his intake of food you will need to gradually reduce the milk offered at one feed until you eventually drop a milk feed. Lunch is usually a good time to do this. You will still need to offer your baby a drink and this should be cooled boiled water in a cup or beaker. Avoid using mineral water as sometimes the mineral contents are unsuitable for babies.

does teething affect my baby's eating?

The age at which babies begin to teethe and the rate at which their teeth come through differs greatly but teething usually starts any time from six months (although very occasionally a baby is actually born with a tooth or two!). Teething can be painful and it may make him irritable and he may become fussier about what he eats during this time.

If he is eating finger foods you can offer chilled, steamed carrot sticks and other vegetables. Never leave your baby unsupervised when eating in case they bite big chunks off which could cause them to choke. If your baby is over six months you can offer chilled yoghurts and fruit purées for pudding, which will also be very soothing for sore gums.

This phase will pass. In the meantime try not to make a big issue if there is a refusal to eat.

I think my baby has a sweet tooth; he will eat fruit and sweeter recipes but rejects the savoury ones. what can I do?

You can avoid your baby developing a sweet tooth by offering vegetable purées initially rather than fruit purées and by not mixing in puréed fruit with a vegetable purée. If your baby is offered a fruit purée immediately after refusing a savoury one, he will quickly learn to reject savoury, knowing that fruit will be offered instead. Try offering savoury finger foods.

You can make savoury dishes slightly sweeter by adding the sweeter vegetables like carrot, butternut squash and sweet potato to encourage your baby to eat savoury dishes again. Although these vegetables are sweet, they are not as sweet as fruit and should not encourage a sweet tooth.

Ensure you offer a variety of recipes to your baby; this is important so he doesn't get bored of the same flavours and start refusing them.

why is my baby still waking for a milk feed in the middle of the night, if he is having three meals a day?

If your baby is taking three meals a day and you are ensuring that he is getting a good variety of protein, carbohydrate, fruit and vegetables in his diet as well as taking at least 500–600 ml (1 pt) of milk per day, he should not be waking due to hunger and is probably waking out of habit. You can try offering cooled boiled water instead (be warned: this might not go down too well with your baby if he is expecting milk!) and if your baby is genuinely thirsty, he may drink a little. You will find if you continue to offer water your baby will soon not expect a milk feed and will

feeding your baby

stop waking. There may be other reasons why your baby has woken other than hunger: he may be teething or may be too cold, hot, ill or a have a very wet or dirty nappy.

my baby is refusing all food, what should I do?

There may be several reasons for this behaviour:

❀ If you are starting to wean and your baby is crying and refusing to eat it could be that he is too hungry. Start with some milk first to satisfy his hunger, then try the food, finishing off with the remaining milk feed.

❀ Try to eat with your baby at mealtimes – your baby will see that eating is a pleasurable and sociable experience, taking the attention away from him.

❀ You need to establish whether he really doesn't like a food or whether he is becoming fussy. Try not to offer a sweet food, pudding or biscuit just because you know he will eat it and you are worried about him going hungry otherwise he will quickly learn that a refusal will be rewarded with a dessert.

❀ If your baby still won't eat after gentle persuasion, then remove the food without a fuss. You could offer a small healthy snack, such as fruit, much later. By the next mealtime he will be hungrier. For the next meal try a different recipe.

❀ Offer a varied selection of foods. Don't dismiss a food just because your baby pushes it away. Try it again a couple of days later in a different way served with something else – he may simply have been too full and it is important to have as varied a diet as possible.

❀ Never force-feed a baby. Mealtimes will then become a battleground and your baby will have negative memories of eating.

❀ He may be trying to exert some independence and control by refusing to eat. Try giving him a spoon and letting him feed himself, in between you spoon-feeding.

❀ Dish up small portions to begin with; a large plate of food can be overwhelming.

❀ Try to eat a meal with some friends and their babies – although they are very young they will be absorbing information and watching others' behaviour.

❀ Make sure that everyone feeding your baby follows the same method. If your baby is looked after by a nursery, relative, childminder or nanny you should be adopting the same approach to encourage continuity.

❀ Ask your partner or a relative to feed the baby at mealtimes. It may break the habit and will give you a well needed rest.

❀ Your baby may be refusing food because he is ill or coming down with something.

❀ If the food refusal lasts for a long period or if you are concerned that there is something wrong, you should seek advice from your doctor or health visitor.

when can I introduce cow's milk?

You can use full-fat cow's milk in your baby's cooking, for example when making a cheese sauce, from six months in the second stage of weaning but you cannot give it to your baby as a drink until he is 12 months as it does not provide the correct balance of nutrients.

the best possible start

cooking know-how

Preparing and cooking food for your baby requires a little extra hygiene in the kitchen and perhaps a little investment in some equipment that will help you produce delicious meals in minutes! Here you'll find advice on keeping away unwanted germs and how to making the most of your cooking sessions so that you can make and store enough food to have something to hand when mealtimes come round and there is a hungry little mouth demanding to be fed!

general food hygiene

All babies are born with an immature immune system and during the first year your baby is most vulnerable to viruses and bacteria. An infection could lead to an illness, such as gastro-enteritis, which causes vomiting and diarrhoea. This can rapidly lead to severe dehydration, requiring medical attention.

Residues of food left on feeding equipment are an excellent breeding ground for bacteria. So, although your baby will be putting things in his mouth, such as toys or fingers, it is still important to reduce the risk to your baby by sterilising drinking and feeding equipment, which ensures that all bacteria and spores have been killed. It is recommended that you sterilise bottles for the first 12 months of your baby's life and we would recommend you sterilise all equipment up to 10 months.

You need to sterilise:

✿ All bottles, teats, caps, lids, breast pumps and breast milk containers.

✿ Feeding bowls and plates.

✿ Baby's cutlery.

✿ Soothers and teethers.

how to sterilise

You should wash and then sterilise after every feed. Before sterilising you should:

✿ Rinse food bowls and spoons with warm water to remove excess food particles, then wash in hot water with mild detergent (food equipment should be washed separately to bottles).

✿ Rinse off with fresh water to remove any traces of detergent.

✿ Discard any chipped, split or cracked bottles or teats as damaged areas can harbour germs.

Electric steam sterilisers destroy bacteria using steam heat. The sterilising cycle can take from 8 to 15 minutes. If the lid is kept on after completion of the cycle, then the items stay sterile for between 1 to 24 hours, depending on the model. Take care when removing the lid, as hot steam can burn.

Microwave steam sterilisers also use steam heat to remove bacteria. A typical sterilising cycle takes three to eight minutes, depending on the model. These sterilisers often hold fewer items than their electric equivalents. Check that the steriliser dimensions will fit into your microwave and don't forget that they are not suitable for metal items.

Traditional method involves cold water with a steriliser and uses chemicals, such as Milton, diluted in water to remove bacteria. Place the items in the sterilising solution and completely submerge. You can buy specific containers to sterilise in, alternatively set aside a large tupperware container and ensure the items are completely submerged. After sterilising you may wish to rinse with cooled boiled water.

Top hygiene tips

✿ Wash your hands regularly before and during milk or food preparation in warm soapy water.

✿ Wash your baby's or toddler's hands before they eat.

✿ Keep your refrigerator at 1–5°C (34–41°F) – buy a fridge thermometer to check.

✿ Keep your freezer at below -18°C (-0.4°F)

✿ Store raw meat on the bottom shelf in the fridge.

✿ Keep work surfaces clean and use antibacterial cleaner.

✿ Regularly wash dish cloths on the hottest cycle or use disposables.

✿ Wash tea towels regularly or ideally air dry utensils and equipment.

✿ Use separate colour-coded chopping boards for raw and cooked meat and vegetables.

✿ Use separate utensils for handling raw and cooked foods.

✿ Make sure all cooking utensils are washed and rinsed to remove any traces of detergent before use.

cook's essentials

You will probably find that you already possess most of the equipment needed for making baby food at home. However, there may be a few items you will need to buy to make your life a little easier.

blenders and food processors

This is one of the essential pieces of equipment needed for puréeing your baby's food to obtain the correct texture, especially during the first stage when you will need to create a smooth purée.

Full size processors and blenders – Ideal when you are cooking large batches. A mini bowl attachment is better for smaller quantities. The Magimix and Kitchen Aid processors are very good and come with smaller bowl attachments. For a considerable investment, the Thermomix is an all-singing, all-dancing machine that weighs, steams/cooks, blends and even reheats, all in one.

Small food processors – These are specially designed for processing baby foods, for example 'Magimix Le Mini' or 'Beaba Babycook Steamer and Blender', which steams, blends, defrosts and reheats. It is compact and easy to clean. It is important to choose a machine that is not too fiddly and, most importantly, easy to clean.

Hand-held blenders – If you buy one piece of equipment, this is the one! These are ideal for puréeing smaller quantities and can also be used for making soups and smoothies. They are easy to clean, easy to store and can also travel with you. You can either purée the food directly in the saucepan or in the plastic beaker provided with the blender. The 'Braun Multiquick Professional Blender' is supplied with a measuring beaker and lid, as well as a chopper attachment. Other recommended blenders are the Kenwood Hand Blender or those made by Bamix.

other useful equipment

Mouli or sieve – Moulis often come with various sized discs so you can alter the texture of your baby food. As well as puréeing, it will remove any indigestible husks from food, such as peas and sweetcorn. A sieve is very useful for removing seeds and fibrous material.

Ice cube trays and freezer containers – The best way to freeze single portions of baby food is in a clean, sterilised ice cube tray. Rubber trays with lids are simplest, as the food is easier to pop out once frozen. We like the 'Beaba Multi-Portion Freezer Tray' and the flexible food freezer tray from www.olimia.com, which is ideal for freezing home-made baby food or breast milk. It has larger portions than standard ice cube trays and has two different-sized compartments for when a baby gets hungrier or for a double portion of his favourite food. It also comes with a lid to prevent cross-contamination, freezer burn or odours. When your baby is eating larger quantities you can freeze in plastic pots with lids.

Plastic zip-lock bags – Once the food has been frozen in the ice cube trays it can be transferred into plastic zip-lock bags before being returned to the freezer for storage. Always label and date before returning to your freezer. These bags are also ideal for transporting sterilised spoons, dummies, etc.

Steamer – A quick, healthy way of cooking vegetables (fewer vitamins are lost during this cooking method). You can buy a multi-tiered steamer which will allow you to cook several vegetables at the same time; a collapsible steamer which will fit in different-sized saucepans or a bamboo one. An alternative to buying a steamer is to use a metal colander or sieve on top of a large saucepan, covered with a lid. Electrical tiered steamers are also available.

Silpat non-stick baking mat – We find this an essential piece of cooking equipment. It keeps all your baking trays clean and is reusable and washable. Simply place the mat on a baking tray instead of using greaseproof paper and when your food is cooked, remove from the silpat baking mat and cool. We use it for baking the muffins and the cheese straws on pages 133–134. It is also an excellent surface for rolling out pastry.

baby essentials

Spoons – Buy plastic spoons for feeding your baby; the ones with soft rubber tips are the best for your little baby's tender gums. Buy at least three or four so you can always have a clean sterilised spoon to hand; as your baby develops he will usually want to hold one while you are feeding him.

Bowls – These should be made of plastic and should be easy to clean and sterilise. There are heat-sensitive bowls that change colour if the food is too hot and ones with suction pads that can be secured to the table and are useful once your baby is attempting to feed himself.

Bibs – An essential part of your weaning kit, they will help to protect your baby's clothes. Initially it's best to use a soft bib – Tommee Tippee do a great milk feeding bib with a thick soft cotton collar which stops any spills going into your baby's neck creases. You can then progress onto the many different bibs that are available.

Feeding cups – Buy one that is easy for your baby to pick up and hold; doesn't leak; has a soft spout and is easy to drink from. Some cups have leak-proof vacuum valves but your baby will have to work hard to get a drink. We like the Heinz Baby Basic range of cups which come in two sizes. They have a 'flexi-soft' plastic spout and are very easy for your baby to use.

High chairs – When you start weaning you can feed your baby in a bouncing chair but as your baby begins to sit up on his own you will need a high chair. Your choice will be guided by space and storage limitations; the comfort of your baby; safety features, such as adequate straps and a five-point harness; and whether it is easy to clean. Some high chairs have a detachable tray, others also feature adjustable height, reclining seats and adjustable footrests.

Booster seats and clip-ons – These are suitable if your baby is sitting well by himself. They can be attached to your dining chairs and allow your child to eat at the table with you. They are more portable than a normal highchair. Clip-on chairs can be attached to a table or a sturdy surface so your baby can be eating alongside you and many fold flat, making them easily transportable.

batch cooking

It is much easier and more economical to cook enough food for a few meals rather than for just one. After you have cooked a recipe, you can chill and then freeze individual portions of the meal. Freezing is a great way to store food – your food will be perfectly safe and suffers minimal nutrient loss.

to freeze purées and baby meals

1 Wash and sterilise the freezer container before use if your baby is less than 10 months old.

2 Cool the purée or meal as quickly as possible. Ice cube trays are intended for use with cold water, so it is safer to cold fill them to prevent chemicals transferring or tainting the food. Place the ice cube tray or pot in a tray or container of cold tap water, without any of the water getting into the purée or meal. Rapid cooling will improve the quality of the product when defrosted and reheated.

3 Cover the freezer container and then transfer to the freezer. Freeze on the same day you have made the purée or meal.

4 If you have used an ice cube tray, then once the purée has frozen, you can pop out the frozen cubes into a clean dish and then tip them into a zip-lock bag. Seal, label with the name of the recipe and date and return to the freezer.

Storage

You should store in a freezer running at -18°C (-0.4°F). You can buy a thermometer to check the temperature. Freeze in suitable containers, for example ice cube trays or plastic pots with lids suitable for freezing. Do not freeze in glass containers.

to reheat baby meals

Whether the food has been defrosted or not it must be thoroughly reheated to piping hot.

1 Place the food in a pan or microwave dish and reheat until cooked through.

2 Stir thoroughly to ensure there are no 'hot spots': this is particularly important when using a microwave.

3 Always check the temperature of the food before you feed your baby. You could do this by either putting a small amount on the inner part of your wrist (which is more sensitive to heat than your hand) or trying a small amount yourself using a separate spoon.

4 Once the food has been reheated it should be served immediately; do not keep and then reheat again. Do not refreeze any thawed food and discard any uneaten food.

defrosting

Ideally take the food out of the freezer the night before and defrost with a cover on in the fridge. Alternatively, reheat from frozen but allow more time and reheat on a lower heat.

feeding your baby 47

Sing a song
of sixpence,
a pocket
full of rye,
four and
twenty
blackbirds
baked in a pie.

part 2
truuuly scrumptious recipes

recipe notes

The following recipes take you from simple first stage purées, through delicious flavour combinations to second stage recipes that will have your baby beating their spoon for more!

portion size

When you begin weaning your baby will be starting with 1–2 teaspoons or 1 ice cube of purée. By the end of the first week you will gradually need to increase the amount given. If your baby still seems hungry after you have given him food you can offer him a little more. You will also need to move gradually from giving him food at one mealtime, to two and then three. All babies are different and will go at their own pace so try not to compare too much with your friends' babies. If you have any worries discuss them with your health visitor or doctor.

note on the recipes

- All milk should be full-fat and organic, if possible.
- All butter should be unsalted, unless otherwise specified.
- All apples are eating apples NOT cooking apples.
- All eggs are large, unless otherwise specified.

All of our recipes are average-sized portions and you may find your baby will eat less or more of each portion.

food allergies and intolerances

The number of allergies reported has escalated in recent years, they are believed to affect one in 20 children under the age of four. If parents or other members of your family suffer from allergies, there is an increased risk that your baby will. The good news is that most babies and children who suffer from allergies grow out of them.

Many of our recipes are already appropriate for babies with allergies. We have suggested the use of olive oil instead of butter to avoid the milk and lactose issues. Other substitutes are as follows:

❀ Change from cow's milk to rice milk for cooking. There are a number of companies producing rice milks which are widely available, or try oat milk, available from health food stores.

❀ Use gluten-free flours, such as rice flour.

❀ Rice pasta is gluten-free. It has a softer texture when cooked but works well. It is fairly widely available and is now made in all different shapes and sizes.

❀ Check all product labels if you are buying ready-made foods and contact your doctor and support groups for advice.

no added salt stocks

It is really important not to use stock cubes when cooking for your baby, as they contain high levels of salt. You can either make your own delicious stocks, or use the Truuuly Scrumptious ready-made varieties, available from www.bathorganicbabyfood.co.uk.

vegetable stock

Makes about 1.4 l (2½ pt)
This easy to make vegetable stock is perfect for adding to any recipe you make for your baby.

2 carrots
1 parsnip
half a small swede
1 onion
1 leek
3 peppercorns
1 large bay leaf
1 bag of bouquet garni
1.75 l (3 pt) water

1 Wash and prepare the vegetables. Peel the carrots, parsnip, swede and onion. Slice the leek in half lengthways and wash.

2 Put vegetables and herbs in a large pan. Add the water and bring to the boil. Reduce the heat and simmer for about 1½ hours, topping up with water if necessary.

3 Remove from the heat and strain the liquid, discarding the vegetables and herbs.

4 Cool quickly and place in the fridge. The stock will be ready for you to use either for baby food or soups. You can, at this stage, freeze in containers to use for future recipes (see page 47).

chicken stock

Makes about 1.4 l (2½ pt)
This stock is perfect for adding to any recipe you make for your baby in the second stage of weaning.

2 carrots
1 parsnip
half a small swede
1 onion
1 leek
1 chicken carcass
3 peppercorns
1 large bay leaf
1 bag of bouquet garni
1.75 l (3 pt) water

1 Prepare the vegetables as for the vegetable stock.

2 Put the vegetables, chicken carcass and herbs in a large pan. Add the water and bring to the boil. Reduce the heat and simmer for about four hours, topping up with water if necessary.

3 Remove from the heat and strain, discarding the vegetables, carcass and herbs.

4 Cool quickly and place in the fridge. Once the stock has been chilled for a few hours or overnight it will have formed a layer of fat on the surface. You can remove this and then the stock will be ready for you to use either for baby food or soups. You can, at this stage, freeze it in containers to use for future recipes (see page 47).

vegetable & fruit preparation

Baby meals sometimes require slightly different food preparation techniques to ensure that it is safe and hygienic to consume. In general, always wash and peel before cooking.

vegetables

Beetroot: Buy fresh, uncooked beetroot – ideally buy a bunch of small summer beetroot. Prepare by leaving the trailing root intact but trim any green stalk down to leaves about 2.5 cm (1 inch) at the top. Wash the beetroot thoroughly in cold water, leave the skin on. Simmer for 20–30 minutes until soft. The skin should be peeled away after cooking and the stalk and root removed.

Broccoli: Wash a head of broccoli and then divide into small florets, removing any tough stalks and leaves.

Brussel sprouts: Wash the sprouts thoroughly in cold water. Trim any damaged outer leaves and cut off a small amount of the stem. There's no need to make a cross incision in the stalk.

Butter beans: Canned are easier to prepare but try to buy organic as they do not contain sulphite preservative. Rinse before use. If using dried, soak in water for 5 hours and drain. Boil in water for 10 minutes, and then simmer for 1–1½ hours until tender. Drain before use.

Butternut squash: Using a large sharp knife, cut the squash in half across the middle so you are left with two pieces; the bulbous end and the longer, thinner piece. Take the thinner piece and slice off the top. Place upright on the chopping board and slice down, removing the skin with a knife. Repeat with the bulbous end, then cut it in half and then quarter. Remove the seeds and fibrous flesh with a knife. Chop all the flesh.

Cabbage: Discard any damaged outer leaves, cut into wedges, discard the hard core then shred or slice thinly. Wash well in cold water.

Carrots: Remove the ends, wash and peel the outer skin. Slice as required.

Cauliflower: Cut away the green outer leaves. Cut the head into florets, discarding the centre stem and wash before use.

Courgette: Remove the ends and wash well before slicing as required.

Herbs: Fresh herbs can be bought either in a packet or in soil tubs. Fresh, ready-picked herbs should be kept in the fridge and used as quickly as possible (within two to three days). Herbs in soil tubs will last longer. Dried herbs have a more concentrated flavour so you need to reduce the amount you use. As a guideline, replace 1 tbsp of fresh herbs with 1 tsp of dried.

Leeks: Cut off the root and as much as the green tops as look tough. Cut a lengthways slit halfway through the leeks or cut very large leeks lengthways in half and wash. Remove the tough outer layer, slice and wash well in a colander. It is best to use the white part of the leek as the green section can be tougher.

Mushrooms: Wipe with a damp cloth or kitchen roll. Do not peel unless skin is damaged. Trim a thin slice off the end of the root.

Onions: Cut a thin slice off the top of the onion. Remove the dry papery skin and peel off any slightly soft layers. Cut in half from top to bottom, hold the onion by the root and slice and then chop, discard the root.

Parsnip: Remove the ends, wash and peel. Slice as required.

Peas: Fresh peas need to be eaten very soon after harvesting as their quality deteriorates in hours rather than days. Split the pods and remove the peas. Rinse before use. Frozen peas are recommended for the following recipes as they are picked and frozen within hours, retaining their nutritional content.

Potatoes: Peel as thinly as possible, as most of the vitamins are contained in or just under the skin. Rinse under cold water. Cut and dice.

We like to use the variety called 'Maris Piper'. They have a light yellow skin and flesh and a mild pleasant taste. They have a firm texture when cooked and are very versatile; they can be used for baking, roasting and boiling. They are 'floury' in texture rather than waxy.

Spinach: Wash well in several changes of water to remove all grit, alternatively you can buy it ready washed, or use frozen. Remove any coarse stalks or tough centre ribs.

Swede: Cut off each end of the swede and peel. Wash in cold water.

Sweetcorn: For fresh sweetcorn, remove the outer leaves and silky threads. Trim the ends. Either cook whole or remove the husks with a sharp knife, cutting down the length of the cob. For canned sweetcorn, buy in unsalted or unsweetened water and drain before use. You can also use frozen sweetcorn.

Sweet potato: Peel with a potato peeler and cut off the ends, rinse under cold water to remove any dirt left behind from peeling. The sweet potato flesh is pinky orange in colour. Slice and dice before use.

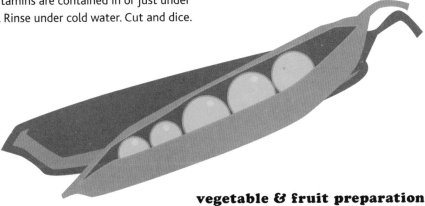

vegetable & fruit preparation

Apricots: For fresh apricots, wash and peel, then cut in half and remove the stones. For canned, buy in unsweetened juice. For dried, you can buy two varieties of dried apricots; there are soft and 'ready to eat' ones or completely dried ones. If you use the completely dried variety you will need to use more water when re-hydrating them. The soft and ready to eat variety will weigh more than the dried variety.

Choose an organic variety of dried apricots which will not have been preserved with sulphur dioxide (which has been known to provoke extreme allergic reactions). The sulphur dioxide makes the apricot more orange; organic ones are darker in colour.

Apple: Wash, peel and core before slicing as required.

Avocado: Halve the avocado lengthways, separate the halves and remove the stone. Peel and remove the flesh.

Keep under-ripe fruit at room temperature or warmer to aid ripening. Store ripe avocados (which are soft when you gently push the skin) in the fridge.

Figs: Fresh figs have a sharp woody stem and this must be removed before cooking. Non-organic figs often contain preservatives. Only remove the skin if it is tough. Dried ready-to-eat and completely dried figs will need to be placed in a pan of boiling water and simmered gently for 5–8 minutes before adding to a recipe.

Kiwi fruit: Peel thinly; a knife is easier than a potato peeler. Cut off both ends. One of the ends will contain a sharp pointed end (soft to touch) which should be removed with a knife. Rinse the fruit before use.

Mangoes: When ripe, mangoes should feel slightly soft if gently squeezed and have a fragrant smell. Allow mangoes to ripen at room temperature, and then refrigerate.

Prepare over a bowl or plate to collect the delicious juice. With a sharp, small knife slice the mango lengthways either side of the stone. If you are using the mango for puréeing or cooking, scoop out the flesh with a spoon. Slice away the remaining strip around the stone and remove the skin.

If the mango is to be eaten raw, slice the mango lengthways on either side of the stone. Hold one of the slices, flesh side up, and cut a criss-cross pattern into the flesh right down to the skin, but not through the skin. Now turn inside out and cut away the cubes of mango.

Melon: Cut in half and remove the seeds with a spoon. Now remove the flesh away from the skin with a spoon or knife and cut or slice as required.

Peaches and nectarines: To peel, first dip in boiling water to loosen the skin. Plunge quickly into cold water. Halve lengthways to remove the stone.

Pear: Wash, peel and core before slicing as required.

meal planner

The following table is a guide only, as all babies develop at different rates and may also be weaned at different times. Your baby may have an extra milk feed in the day and later on may also be having a mid-morning or mid-afternoon snack.

Remember it is important to offer new foods one at a time so that your baby gets used to different tastes and textures; allowing a few days on a new food will also enable you to detect any adverse or allergic reactions.

weaning: getting started

	early morning	breakfast	lunch	tea	bedtime
week 1	Milk feed	Milk feed	Milk feed *1–2 tsp baby rice or simple vegetable purée* Remainder of milk feed	Milk feed	Milk feed
week 2	Milk feed	Milk feed	Milk feed *3–4 tsp vegetable purée* Remainder of milk feed	Milk feed	Milk feed
week 3/4	Milk feed	Milk feed *Puréed fruit with baby rice* Remainder of milk feed	Milk feed *Vegetable combination purées* Remainder of milk feed	Milk feed	Milk feed

continued over

	early morning	breakfast	lunch	tea	bedtime
week 5/6	Milk feed	Milk feed *Puréed fruit mixed with baby rice or baby cereal* Remainder of milk feed	Milk feed *Savoury purée* Remainder of milk feed	Milk feed *Savoury purée* Remainder of milk feed	Milk feed
week 7/8	Milk feed	*Baby cereal or porridge* Milk feed	*Savoury purée followed by fruit purée* Smaller milk feed in a cup	*Savoury purée* Milk feed	Milk feed
week 9/10	Milk feed	*Porridge, Weetabix or baby cereal* Milk feed	*Savoury purée followed by fruit purée.* Water in a cup	*Savoury purée followed by fruit purée or yoghurt* Milk feed	Milk feed
week 10/11	Milk feed	*Porridge, Weetabix or baby cereal followed by fruit* Milk in a cup	*Savoury purée followed by fruit purée* Water in a cup	*Savoury purée followed by fruit purée or yoghurt* Milk in a cup	Milk feed

 truuuly scrumptious recipes

easy-peasy vegetable purées

Once your baby has shown signs that he is ready for weaning (see page 29) and he has reached at least 17 weeks then you can start to introduce these delicious simple vegetable purées. The orange vegetables, like carrot and sweet potato, are ideal first vegetables as they are naturally sweet, highly nutritious and are sure to be gobbled up quickly by your baby.

Once your baby has tried a few single vegetable purées you can start combining them for variety. Try carrot, parsnip and swede, or sweet potato, carrot and broccoli – both huge favourites with our babies!

carrot makes 2 – 3 portions

Carrots are an excellent ingredient to make into your baby's first purée. They should be puréed until completely smooth and fairly runny in texture to get your baby used to swallowing.

2 carrots (about 300 g/10½ oz in total), sliced

1. Place the carrots in a pan and just cover with boiling water. Bring to the boil then reduce the heat and simmer for 10–15 minutes until soft. Alternatively, steam until the carrots are soft – about 15 minutes or.
2. Place in a blender and blend to a smooth purée.
3. Serve one portion. Cover and chill the remainder and use within 24 hours or chill then freeze in small portions (see page 47).

butternut squash makes 4 – 5 portions

Butternut squash is a good source of vitamin A and betacarotene. The smooth, velvety texture and bright colour make it a top favourite with babies. All of our babies loved this one (as did Topsy!).

half a medium butternut squash (about 500 g/16 oz), diced

1. Place the diced butternut squash in a pan and just cover with boiling water. Bring to the boil then reduce the heat and simmer for 10–15 minutes until soft. Alternatively, steam until soft.
2. Cool slightly then place in a blender and blend to a smooth purée.
3. Serve one portion. Cover and chill the remainder and use within 24 hours or chill then freeze in portions (see page 47).

truuuly scrumptious recipes

parsnip makes 2 – 3 portions

For the best flavour, use parsnips in season. Parsnips can produce quite a dry purée so you may need to slacken the purée by adding more vegetable stock.

2 parsnips (about 300 g/10½ oz in total), diced
60 ml (2 fl oz) No Added Salt Vegetable Stock (see page 51)
or reserved cooking water

1. Place the parsnips in a pan and just cover with boiling water. Bring to the boil then reduce the heat and simmer for 10–15 minutes until soft. Alternatively, steam until the parsnips are soft – about 15 minutes.
2. Place the cooked parsnip in a blender with the vegetable stock or reserved cooking water and blend to a smooth purée.
3. Serve one portion. Cover and chill the remainder and use within 24 hours or chill then freeze in portions (see page 47).

swede makes 2 portions

Swede makes a good starter recipe as it is easy to prepare and has a lovely flavour. (It can also be successfully combined with other vegetables when your baby is ready for more complex flavours.)

half a small swede (about 250 g/9 oz), cubed
20–30 ml (1 fl oz) No Added Salt Vegetable Stock (see page 51)
or reserved cooking water

1. Place the swede in a pan and just cover with boiling water. Bring to the boil then reduce the heat and simmer for 10–15 minutes until soft. Alternatively, place in a steamer and steam for about 15 minutes or until the swede is soft.
2. Place the swede in a blender with the vegetable stock or reserved cooking water and blend to a smooth purée.
3. Serve one portion. Cover and chill the remainder and use within 24 hours or chill then freeze in portions (see page 47).

easy-peasy vegetable purées 59

sweet potato

This is a big favourite with little ones! It has a sweet flavour and is much less starchy than ordinary potato so it produces an excellent puréed texture which is deep orange in colour. We often make sweet potato mash for the family to top pies or as a side dish to make a change from ordinary mashed potatoes.

1 medium sweet potato (about 300 g/10½ oz), diced
100 ml (3½ fl oz) No Added Salt Vegetable Stock (see page 51)
or reserved cooking water

1   Place the sweet potato in a pan and just cover with boiling water. Bring to the boil then reduce the heat and simmer for 10–15 minutes until soft. Alternatively, place in a steamer and steam for about 15 minutes or until the sweet potato is soft.

2   Put the sweet potato and the stock into a blender and blend until you have a smooth purée.

3   Serve one portion. Cover and chill the remainder and use within 24 hours or chill then freeze in portions (see page 47).

butternut squash
& broccoli

Broccoli and butternut squash provide a nutritious dose of iron and vitamin C, along with betacarotene. Broccoli has a strong flavour and works well mixed with other vegetables, giving the purée an appealing, speckled appearance.

270 g (9½ oz) butternut squash (about 115 g/4 oz once
peeled and seeded), diced
55 g (2 oz) broccoli florets

 truuuly scrumptious recipes

1. Place the butternut squash and broccoli into a pan and just cover with boiling water. Bring to the boil then reduce the heat and simmer for about 15 minutes until the vegetables are soft. Alternatively, steam for about 15 minutes until soft.
2. Place the vegetables in a blender and purée to a smooth consistency.
3. Serve one portion. Cover and chill the remainder and use within 24 hours or chill then freeze in portions (see page 47).

carrot & courgette makes 2 – 3 portions

Courgettes can be rather bitter on their own. Combine them with a sweeter vegetable, such as carrots, to balance the flavour and you have a tasty purée.

2 carrots (about 250 g/9 oz in total), sliced
half a courgette (about 115 g/4 oz), sliced

1. Place the carrots in a pan and just cover with boiling water. Bring to the boil then reduce the heat and simmer for 5 minutes. Add the sliced courgettes and simmer for a further 10 minutes or until both vegetables are cooked. Alternatively, place the vegetables in a steamer in the same order and steam until soft.
2. Place the cooked vegetables in a blender and purée to a smooth consistency.
3. Serve one portion. Cover and chill the remainder and use within 24 hours or chill then freeze in portions (see page 47).

easy-peasy vegetable purées

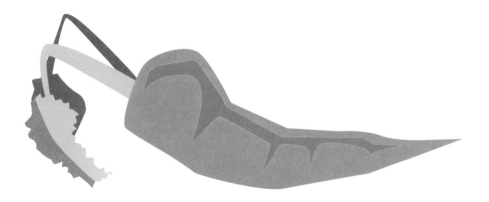

carrot, parsnip & swede *makes 3 – 5 portions*

This is a classic combination of root vegetables. It was a favourite with all of our children when they were babies and, in fact, it won an award in the Soil Association Organic Food Awards in 2002!

1 carrot (about 115 g/4 oz), sliced
100 g (3½ oz) parsnip, diced
85 g (3 oz) swede, diced
No Added Salt Vegetable Stock (see page 51)
or reserved cooking water

1 Place the vegetables in a pan and just cover with boiling water. Bring to the boil then reduce the heat and simmer for 10–15 minutes. Alternatively, steam until soft.

2 Purée the vegetables in a blender, gradually adding small amounts of cooking water or salt-free vegetable stock to obtain a smooth purée.

3 Serve one portion. Cover and chill the remainder and use within 24 hours or chill then freeze in portions (see page 47).

potato, courgette & pea *makes 4 portions*

This was one of our first recipes and it continues to be very popular with the young babies. It has a lovely creamy texture and a well balanced flavour – you will be able to taste each vegetable.

1 large baking potato (about 250 g/9 oz), diced
half a courgette (about 150 g/5 oz), sliced
75 g (2½ oz) frozen peas or petit pois
60 ml (2 fl oz) No Added Salt Vegetable Stock (see page 51)
*   or reserved cooking water*

1. Place the potato in a pan and cover with boiling water. Bring to the boil and cook for about 10 minutes.
2. Add the peas and courgettes to the potatoes and cook for a further 5 minutes until the potatoes are cooked. Alternatively, you can place the courgettes on their own in a steamer and steam for about 5–6 minutes until cooked through.
3. Place all of the cooked vegetables with the vegetable stock in a mouli in order to remove the pea husk. If you use petit pois you may be able to blend all the ingredients together in a blender, as the husk is not as tough.
4. Serve one portion. Cover and chill the remainder and use within 24 hours or chill then freeze in portions (see page 47).

sweet potato & parsnip
makes 4 – 5 portions

Parsnip and sweet potatoes make a lovely smooth texture and are a good first combination to try. Babies who are not keen on plain parsnip may prefer it blended with a sweeter tasting vegetable.

1 medium sweet potato (about 300 g/10½ oz), diced
1 parsnip (about 150 g/5½ oz), diced
No Added Salt Vegetable Stock (see page 51) or reserved cooking water

1   Place the sweet potato and parsnip in a pan, add enough boiling water just to cover the vegetables. Bring to the boil. Reduce the heat then simmer for 10–12 minutes until the vegetables are soft. Drain, reserving a little cooking water. Alternatively, steam until soft.
2   Place the cooked sweet potato and parsnip in a blender. Add a little stock or cooking water and blend to a smooth purée.
3   Serve one portion. Cover and chill the remainder and use within 24 hours or chill and freeze in portions (see page 47).

   truuuly scrumptious recipes

sweet potato, carrot & broccoli makes 3 – 5 portions

This is a supercharged combination, full of essential vitamins and minerals, that will provide a boost for growing babies. They'll love the bright colour and naturally sweet flavour.

1 sweet potato (about 280 g/10 oz), diced
1 carrot (about 100 g/3½ oz), sliced
85 g (3 oz) broccoli florets
130 ml (4½ fl oz) No Added Salt Vegetable Stock (see page 51)
or reserved cooking water

1   Place the sweet potato in a pan and cover with boiling water. Bring back to the boil, reduce the heat and simmer for 8 minutes. Add the carrot and simmer for a further 6 minutes. Finally, add the broccoli and simmer for 5 minutes until all the vegetables are tender. Alternatively, add the vegetables to a steamer and steam in the same order until all the vegetables are cooked.

2   Purée the vegetables in a blender, adding the vegetable stock or cooking water to obtain a smooth purée.

3   Serve one portion. Cover and chill the remainder and use within 24 hours or chill then freeze in portions (see page 47).

easy-peasy vegetable purées

five veg medley

Once you have tried vegetables individually you can start blending them. You can alter the combination or amounts and change the ingredients according to what's in season. You can taste subtle flavours from all of the vegetables in this purée which was a hit with our babies.

> 1 carrot (about 125g/4½ oz), sliced
> half a courgette (about 115 g/4 oz), sliced
> 1 small sweet potato (about 170 g/6 oz), diced
> 75 g (2½ oz) cauliflower florets
> 45 g (1½ oz) broccoli florets
> No Added Salt Vegetable Stock (see page 51) or reserved
>   cooking water (optional)

1 Place the carrots in a pan and cover with boiling water. Bring to the boil and simmer for 5 minutes. Then add the sweet potato, broccoli and cauliflower and simmer for a further 5 minutes. Finally add the courgettes and simmer for 5 minutes. Alternatively, you can place the vegetables in the same order in a steamer and steam until tender.

2 Add the cooked vegetables to a blender and purée either until completely smooth or leave with some texture if your baby is ready.

3 At this stage if you wish you can add a little stock or reserved cooking water to the purée to obtain the right consistency for your baby.

4 Serve one portion. Cover and chill the remainder and use within 24 hours or chill then freeze in portions (see page 47).

roasted vegetable medley makes 6 ~ 7 portions

Packed with vitamin A, this is delicious and a great one to cook while you are cooking a roast for the rest of the family. It also adapts well for older children and adults, making a tasty pasta sauce or a delicious soup with the addition of more stock.

half a small butternut squash (about 400 g/14 oz), seeded
1 small sweet potato (about 180 g/6½ oz)
2 carrots (about 300 g/10½ oz in total), sliced
140 g (5 oz) swede, diced
55 g (2 oz) broccoli florets
100 ml (3½ fl oz) No Added Salt Vegetable Stock
(see page 51)

1 Preheat the oven to 200°C/400°F/gas mark 6.

2 Place the unpeeled butternut squash and sweet potato on a baking tray and bake in the centre of the oven for 40–45 minutes until cooked.

3 Place the carrots and swede in a pan and just cover with boiling water. Bring back to the boil then reduce the heat and simmer for 10 minutes. Add the broccoli to the pan and simmer for a further 6–8 minutes until all the vegetables are tender. Alternatively, steam the vegetables in a steamer in the same order until soft.

4 Scoop out the flesh from the cooked sweet potato and butternut squash and discard the skin.

5 Add all the vegetables to a blender with the vegetable stock. Purée to the desired consistency for your baby.

6 Serve one portion and chill the remainder and use within 24 hours or chill and freeze in portions (see page 47).

easy-peasy vegetable purées

fantastic fruit purées

Once your baby has got used to a few savoury tastes you can start to introduce some delicious fruit purées. For first fruit tastes the best ones to start with are the cooked apple or pear (delicious mixed with a little baby rice), mashed banana or avocado. You can then move onto the fruit combinations and uncooked, puréed ripe fruit.

These fruit recipes are quick and easy to make and you and your baby will find that there is nothing quite like home-cooked fruit purées! Our older children, both aged seven, still enjoy these fruit purées either as a pudding or mixed into a home-made smoothie. You could try them and boost your own five-a-day intake too!

apple makes 2-3 portions

This is a perfect first fruit recipe that is enjoyed by all babies. You could mix with baby rice and breast milk or formula to make a creamy variation. Choose sweet, juicy eating apples.

3 apples (about 370 g/13 oz in total), peeled, cored and sliced

1. Place the sliced apples in a pan and just cover with boiling water. Bring to the boil then reduce to a simmer. Simmer for about 10 minutes until the apple is soft. Drain. Alternatively, steam until soft – about 10 minutes.
2. Place the apple in a blender and purée to a smooth consistency.
3. You can serve on its own or add a little of your baby's usual milk mixed with baby rice. Cover and chill the remainder of the apple and use within 24 hours or chill then freeze in portions (see page 47).

if you find fibres in your apple purée, simply sieve to remove and create a super smooth consistency

pear makes 2-3 portions

Avoid pears with a gritty texture, such as Conference – try Anjou or Williams instead. As your baby gets older you can mash peeled raw pears without cooking, so long as they are really ripe and juicy.

***2 large ripe pears (about 340 g/12 oz in total),
peeled, cored and sliced***

1 Place the pears in a pan and cover with boiling water. Bring to the boil then reduce to a simmer. Simmer for about 5–10 minutes until the pear is soft. Drain. Alternatively, steam for about 5–10 minutes until soft.

2 Place the pear in a blender and purée to a smooth consistency.

3 You can serve this on it's own or mixed with a little baby rice; sometimes pear purée can be a little runny so the baby rice will make it thicker.

4 Cover and chill the remainder of the purée and use within 24 hours or chill then freeze in portions (see page 47).

banana makes 1 portion

This has to be the simplest purée there is. It is so easy to prepare and is ideal for when you are out and about – it even has built-in biodegradable packaging! Never use under ripe bananas; choose ones which are beginning to brown on the skin.

half a medium banana

1 Peel the banana and either mash well with a clean fork or place in a blender and blend to a smooth consistency.

2 Serve one portion. [Cover and chill the remainder in the fridge and use within 24 hours.] This will mix well with other fruit.

This purée is not suitable for freezing.

truuuly scrumptious recipes

avocado makes 2 portions

Avocados, like bananas, will discolour when exposed to air over a period of time, so prepare just before use and eat the other half yourself in a salad. This lovely green purée is packed full of nutrients and is a great source of vitamin E.

half a ripe avocado

1 Scoop out the flesh and mash with a clean fork or place in a blender and blend to a smooth consistency.
2 Serve. Avocado is delicious on its own or mixed with a little mashed banana or puréed pear.

This purée is not suitable for freezing.

mango makes 2 portions

Tropical fruit, such as mangoes, are ideal in the first stage of weaning, as they provide a good dose of vitamin C at an age when citrus fruit should be avoided. This vibrant purée has instant baby appeal.

half a ripe mango

1 Scoop out the flesh with a spoon and purée in a food processor or blender.
2 Sometimes mangoes can be quite fibrous, so you may wish to sieve the purée to remove the fibres before serving.

fantastic fruit purées

melon makes 2 – 3 portions

Sweet, juicy melons have a wonderful aroma and flavour in season. Simple to prepare, this delicious purée mixes well with baby rice to make a sweet treat .

half a small cantaloupe melon (about 450 g/1 lb),
seeded and diced
2 heaped tbsp baby rice

1 Place the prepared melon in a blender and purée. After puréeing you will need to add the baby rice to thicken the mixture.
2 Serve one portion. Cover and chill the remainder and use within 48 hours.

This purée is not suitable for freezing.

apple, pear & cinnamon makes 2 – 3 portions

Just a pinch of cinnamon complements the classic combination of apple and pear and reminds us of Christmas. Cinnamon is good for the immune system and has antibacterial qualities.

2 large apples (about 300 g/10½ oz in total), peeled, cored
and sliced
1 large pear (about 200 g/7 oz), peeled, cored and sliced
a large pinch of ground cinnamon

1 Place the apples in a pan and add enough boiling water to cover the fruit. Bring to the boil, then reduce the heat and simmer for about five minutes.
2 Add the pears and simmer for a further five minutes until all the fruit is soft. Drain. Alternatively, place the fruit in a steamer and steam the fruit in the same order until soft.
3 Place the fruit and ground cinnamon in a blender; blend to a smooth purée.
4 Serve one portion. Cover and chill the remainder and use within 24 hours or chill then freeze in portions (see page 47).

truuuly scrumptious recipes

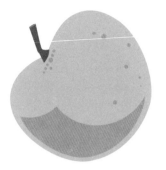
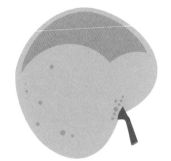

apple, peach & banana makes 4 – 5 portions

When fresh peaches are out of season you can use canned, which don't require cooking. Buy them in natural unsweetened juice and add the juice back into the purée to make a smoothie for older children or treat yourself!

> *3 apples (about 370 g/13 oz in total), peeled, cored and sliced*
> *1 peach or nectarine (about 140 g/5 oz), peeled, stoned and chopped or canned peach slices (in natural juice without added sugar), drained and juice reserved*
> *1 banana (about 125 g/4½ oz)*

1 Place the apples in a pan and cover with boiling water. Bring to the boil then reduce the heat and simmer for five minutes.

2 Add the peach to the apple and simmer for a further five minutes. Drain. Alternatively, place the fruit in the steamer in the same order and steam until soft.

3 Peel the banana and place in the blender with the cooked apples and peaches. Purée to the desired consistency for your baby.

4 Serve one portion. Cover and chill the remainder and use within 24 hours or chill then freeze in portions (see page 47).

fantastic fruit purées

apple & apricot

Choose lovely English apples in season. Our favourite variety is the delicious Pink Lady but we also like Braeburn and Gala. Remember to use organic apricots which will be darker in colour and do not contain sulphur dioxide. Apricots are a fantastic source of iron which will be more easily absorbed by the presence of vitamin C contained in the apples. This recipe won us the runners up award in the 'Dried Fruit Awards' in 2003.

3 medium apples (about 370 g/13 oz in total), peeled, cored
 and sliced
30 g (1 oz) soft and ready to eat organic apricots (about 4–5), rinsed
60 ml (2 fl oz) boiling water

1 Place the apples in a pan and cover with boiling water. Bring to the boil then reduce the heat and simmer for 10 minutes until the apples are soft. Alternatively, steam for 10 minutes until soft.

2 Meanwhile place the apricots in a pan with the boiling water. Simmer for five minutes until the apricots have been rehydrated.

3 Place the cooked apples and apricots in a blender and purée to a smooth consistency.

4 Serve one portion. Cover and chill the remainder and use within 24 hours or chill then freeze in portions (see page 47).

choose organic apricots that are darker in colour and don't contain the preservative sulphur dioxide

peach & baby rice

This is a beautiful delicately flavoured purée. It works best with fresh peaches so wait until they are in season and choose luscious ripe flavoursome fruit.

3 ripe peaches or nectarines (about 400 g/14 oz), peeled, stoned and sliced
1 tbsp baby rice

1. Place the peaches in a pan with enough boiling water to cover the fruit. Bring back to the boil then reduce the heat and simmer for five minutes. Drain. Alternatively, steam for about five minutes.
2. Put the peaches in a blender and purée to a smooth consistency. Add the baby rice.
3. You can serve the puréed peaches on their own or once your baby has had some dairy foods you can stir in a spoonful of natural yoghurt.
4. Cover and chill the remainder and use within 24 hours or chill then freeze in portions (see page 47).

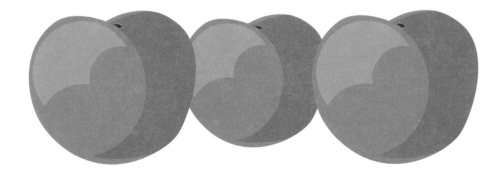

fantastic fruit purées

perfect pasta & scrumptious vegetables

stage 2

You can begin the second stage of weaning once your baby has been eating simple vegetable and fruit purées for a few weeks. Although milk is still very important in your baby's diet, now is the time to start introducing foods with more taste and texture. Some babies will take to the new textures with no problems, others may need to progress more slowly. The following recipes provide a variety of nutrients and will introduce your baby to protein, gluten and dairy. You will still need to be careful and introduce new foods gradually to watch for any allergic reactions. If you need to avoid any of these food types you can substitute certain ingredients with alternatives (see page 50).

peas with garlic & crème fraîche

It is perfectly safe to introduce garlic to your babies diet. What's more, babies enjoy strong flavours. Use very fresh or frozen peas for maximum nutritional value in this delicious, bright green purée that appeals to the eyes as well as developing taste buds.

> *1 small clove of garlic*
> *180 g (6½ oz) frozen peas or petit pois*
> *1 tbsp crème fraîche*
> *reserved cooking water*

1. Remove the skin from the garlic and place in a pan with the peas. Add boiling water to cover the peas.
2. Bring to the boil then reduce the heat and simmer for 10 minutes.
3. Place the cooked peas and garlic clove in a blender. Add the crème fraîche and a little of the reserved cooking water. Blend to a smooth purée, use a mouli if you need to remove tough skins.
4. This delicious purée can be served on its own or stirred into some cooked pasta. Serve one portion. Cover and chill the remainder and use within 24 hours or chill then freeze in portions (see page 47).

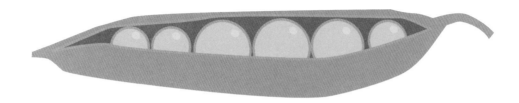

perfect pasta & scrumptious vegetables

beetroot & roast tomato

makes 3 – 4 portions

This delicious purée has instant baby appeal due to its amazing intense colour. It also makes a great pasta sauce for grown-ups with with goats' cheese sprinkled on top. Don't panic at nappy change time – eating beetroot can give you pink urine!

2 beetroots (about 250 g/9 oz in total)
2 large beef tomatoes (about 400 g/14 oz in total)
half a clove of garlic, crushed
olive oil

1. Preheat the oven to 190°C/375°F/Gas Mark 5.
2. Prepare the beetroot (see page 52). Meanwhile cut the beef tomatoes in half horizontally and place on a baking tray skin side down.
3. Spread the crushed garlic across the four tomato halves, drizzle with olive oil and bake in the top of the oven for half an hour.
4. Remove the tomatoes from the oven and peel and discard the skin.
5. Place the cooked tomatoes and cooked beetroot into a blender and purée.
6. Serve one portion. Cover and chill the remainder and use within 24 hours or chill then freeze in portions (see page 47).

 truuuly scrumptious recipes

Quinoa is an excellent source of high-quality protein. Combined with potato and spinach, it is a filling dish providing a good balance of nutrients that will fuel your baby throughout the afternoon.

30 g (1 oz) butter or 1½ tbsp olive oil
half a small onion (about 55 g/2 oz), finely chopped
1 large potato (about 400 g/14 oz), diced
550 ml (19 fl oz) No Added Salt Chicken or Vegetable Stock
   (see page 51)
2 heaped dessert spoons of flaked quinoa
225 g (8 oz) fresh spinach, washed and tough stalks removed

1   Place the butter or oil in a pan on a low heat. Once the butter has melted, add the onion and cook on a low heat for about five minutes until the onions are soft and transparent.

2   Add the potatoes and cook with the onions for a few minutes, stirring constantly.

3   Add half the stock and bring to the boil. Reduce the heat, cover and simmer for 10 minutes stirring occasionally.

4   Add the remainder of the stock and the quinoa. Stir the quinoa in well and bring back to the boil. Reduce the heat, cover and simmer for five minutes.

5   Add the spinach a handful at a time and stir into the mix (once the spinach reaches the heat it will shrink, so don't panic if you think there is far too much spinach!). Cook, covered, on a low heat for 10 minutes.

6   Remove from the heat. You can either put this dish in a blender and blend to the correct consistency for your baby, or mash with a fork, depending on your baby's progress.

7   Serve one portion. Cover and chill the remainder and use within 24 hours or chill then freeze in portions (see page 47).

leek & potato

Babies love this combination and it's simple to prepare. Use Maris Piper potatoes which have a good flavour and nice floury texture – ideal for a perfect purée. With the addition of a little more stock you can turn this into a classic leek and potato soup so that the adults don't miss out!

> *30 g (1 oz) butter*
> *45 g (1½ oz) onion, finely chopped*
> *1 large leek (about 115 g/4 oz), sliced*
> *3 potatoes (about 470 g/16½ oz in total), diced*
> *300 ml (10 fl oz) No Added Salt Vegetable Stock (see page 51)*

1 Melt the butter in a pan on a low heat, then add the onions. Cook gently for about five minutes or until soft and transparent. Then add the leeks and cook for a further five minutes until the leeks have softened.

2 Add the potatoes and cook for about 3–4 minutes, stirring constantly.

3 Add the stock and bring to the boil. Reduce the heat and simmer for about 15 minutes until the potatoes are cooked.

4 Remove from the heat and place the vegetables in a blender and purée to the correct consistency for your baby. You may need to add a little more stock or boiled water if the consistency is too thick for your baby.

5 Serve one portion. Cover and chill the remainder and use within 24 hours or chill then freeze in portions (see page 47).

truuuly scrumptious recipes

ratatouille & quinoa

This richly-flavoured purée is based on the ever versatile tomato – a superfood packed with vitamins and the antioxidant lycopene, which gives it its lush colour. The quinoa adds high quality protein to the dish. You can serve this on its own or stir it into some cooked pasta.

30 g (1 oz) butter or 1½ tbsp olive oil
55 g (2 oz) onion, finely chopped
1 small clove of garlic
2 medium carrots (about 200 g/7 oz in total), thinly sliced
1½ tins chopped tomatoes (600 g/21 oz)
1½ courgettes (about 300 g/10½ oz in total), sliced
85 g (3 oz) broccoli florets
360 ml (12 fl oz) No Added Salt Vegetable Stock (see page 51)
a pinch of mixed dried herbs
4 fresh basil leaves
2 heaped dessert spoons flaked quinoa

1 Place the butter or oil in a pan and melt over a low heat. Add the onions and cook on a low heat for five minutes, then add the garlic and cook for a further few minutes.

2 Add the carrots and cook, covered, for a further 5 minutes, stirring occasionally then add the courgettes and cook for 3–4 minutes.

3 Add the tomatoes, broccoli, stock and mixed herbs and basil. Bring to the boil, reduce the heat, cover and simmer for 15 minutes, stirring occasionally.

4 Add the quinoa, stir well and simmer for a final 10 minutes.

5 Place in a blender and purée to the right consistency for your baby, or alternatively mash with a fork.

6 Serve one portion. Cover and chill the remainder and use within 24 hours or chill then freeze in portions (see page 47).

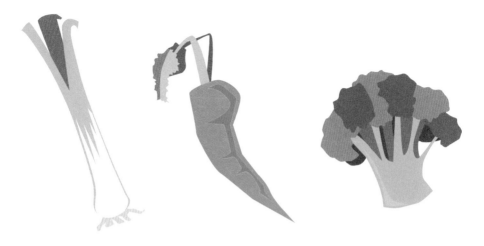

vegetable gratin
makes 4 ~ 5 portions

This is a lovely, fresh-tasting dish; the juices from the vegetables mix with the cheese to form a delicious sauce. This is a versatile recipe which can be eaten on its own or with pasta.

2 carrots (about 225 g/8 oz in total), sliced
140 g (5 oz) broccoli florets
half a small leek, white part only (about 55 g/2 oz), sliced
1 courgette (about 180 g/6½ oz), sliced
55 g (2 oz) mature Cheddar cheese, grated
No Added Salt Vegetable Stock (see page 51) or reserved cooking
  water (optional)

1 Place the carrots in a pan and cover with boiling water. Bring to the boil then reduce the heat and simmer for 10 minutes.

2 Add the broccoli, leek and courgette and simmer for a further 6–8 minutes until all the vegetables are cooked.

3 Alternatively, place the vegetables in a steamer and steam in the same order until all the vegetables are cooked.

4 Add the cooked vegetables to a blender with the cheese and blend to the correct consistency for your baby. You may need to add stock or reserved cooking water to loosen the mixture for him.

5 Serve one portion. Cover and chill the remainder and use within 24 hours or chill then freeze in portions (see page 47).

truuuly scrumptious recipes

cauliflower & broccoli cheese

A nursery favourite, this dish provides calcium from the milk and cheese and vitamin C from the vegetables – nutritious and delicious! Feel free to add additional vegetables, such as carrots or peas, for a tasty variation.

280 g (10 oz) cauliflower florets
160 g (5½ oz) broccoli florets
30 g (1 oz) butter
30 g (1 oz) plain flour
360 ml (12½ fl oz) milk
55 g (2 oz) mature Cheddar cheese, grated

1. Steam the cauliflower and broccoli for about 10–15 minutes until cooked and set aside.
2. Meanwhile melt the butter in a pan on a low heat. Add the flour and stir on a gentle heat. Cook on a low heat for a few minutes until it starts to bubble and resemble honeycomb. Do not overcook at this stage as you will burn the flour.
3. Remove from the heat and gradually add the milk, stirring constantly (you could use a balloon whisk to ensure a smooth sauce).
4. Once all the milk has been added, return the pan to the heat and slowly bring back to the boil, stirring to create a lump-free sauce.
5. Reduce the heat and cook for a few minutes. The sauce will thicken.
6. Remove from the heat and add the grated cheese. Stir until melted.
7. Add the cauliflower and broccoli to a blender with the cheese sauce and blend to the correct consistency for your baby. Alternatively mash with a fork.
8. Serve one portion. Cover and chill the remainder and use within 24 hours or chill then freeze in portions (see page 47).

sweetcorn chowder

This recipe won us the Soil Association Organic Baby Food Award in 2002. We were over the moon and it helped to get us on the map. Babies will love the sunny yellow colour and fantastic taste – and it's easy to make!

15 g (½ oz) butter or 1 tbsp olive oil
30 g (1 oz) onion, finely chopped
1 carrot (about 120 g/4 oz), sliced
1 potato (about 180 g/6½ oz), diced
85 g (3 oz) canned sweetcorn, drained
200 ml (7 fl oz) No Added Salt Vegetable Stock (see page 51)
a pinch of dried mixed herbs

1. Melt the butter or oil in a pan on a low heat. Add the onion and cook on a low heat for about five minutes, stirring frequently. Add the carrot and continue cooking gently until the onion is soft, about 4–5 minutes, stirring to ensure that the carrots and onions do not burn.
2. Add the potato and mixed herbs and cook for a further five minutes, stirring frequently.
3. Add the sweetcorn and stock. Bring to the boil, cover and simmer, stirring occasionally until the potatoes are cooked (about 15–20 minutes).
4. Remove from the heat and put through a mouli on a medium disc to remove the sweetcorn husk.
5. Serve one portion. Cover and chill the remainder and use within 24 hours or freeze in portions (see page 47).

 truuuly scrumptious recipes

lentil bake makes 3 – 4 portions

Lentils are a good source of protein as well as iron, fibre and vitamins. When cooked, the lentils will thicken this mix producing a delicious smooth texture. Add a little more stock and you have a thick soup for yourself to enjoy with a hunk of granary bread as you share this wonderful taste experience with your baby.

15 g (½ oz) butter or 1 tbsp olive oil
30 g (1 oz) onion, finely chopped
85 g (3 oz) leek, sliced
1 carrot (about 150 g/5 oz), sliced
45 g (1½ oz) red lentils
1 potato (about 225 g/8 oz), diced
300 ml (10½ fl oz) No Added Salt Vegetable Stock (see page 51)

1 Melt the butter or oil on a low heat, then add the onion and cook for about five minutes until soft and transparent.

2 Add the leeks and cook for a further 4 minutes.

3 Add the carrots, cover and cook on a low heat, stirring occasionally, for about 8 minutes.

4 Add the lentils and cook, stirring constantly, for about 4 minutes.

5 Finally add the potato and the stock. Bring to the boil then reduce the heat and simmer for about 20 minutes until the potatoes are cooked.

6 Remove from the heat and chop or blend to the desired consistency for your baby.

7 Serve one portion. Cover and chill the remainder and use within 24 hours or chill then freeze in portions (see page 47).

pasta with spinach, watercress & crème fraîche

When heated, crème fraîche makes a ready-made creamy sauce – a great alternative to milk sauce. It is bland in flavour and is best combined with other ingredients, such as tangy watercress, bursting with antioxidants and iron, and nutty Gruyère, which gives a great cheesy texture to the sauce.

85 g (3 oz) dried pasta
100 ml (3½ fl oz) crème fraîche
125 g (4½ oz) spinach, washed and tough stalks removed
30 g (1 oz) watercress, washed and tough stalks removed
a pinch of grated nutmeg
45 g (1½ oz) Gruyère cheese, grated

1 Place the pasta in a pan of water and cook according to the packet instructions.

2 Meanwhile, place the crème fraîche in a pan and melt over a low heat. Add the spinach and watercress and cook on a low heat, stirring occasionally, for about 6–8 minutes until cooked. Add the nutmeg and Gruyère and cook for a further 2–3 minutes.

3 Drain the pasta. Either combine all the ingredients and purée to the desired consistency or, if you are using mini pasta shapes, you can purée the sauce to a smooth purée and pour over the cooked pasta.

4 Serve one portion. Cover and chill the remainder and use within 24 hours or chill then freeze in portions (see page 47).

pasta with five vegetable sauce

makes 7 – 8 portions

This sauce is a tasty way of combining vegetables packed with a range of vitamins. It is an excellent accompaniment to pasta or alternatively add cooked diced chicken to increase the protein content of the meal. Our children love sprinkling grated mature Cheddar on top.

100 g (3½ oz) dried pasta
30 g (1 oz) butter or 1½ tbsp olive oil
55 g (2 oz) onion, finely chopped
1 small clove of garlic, crushed
2 carrots (about 250 g/9 oz in total), sliced
half a red pepper (about 85 g/3 oz), deseeded and diced
half a yellow pepper (about 85 g/3 oz), deseeded and diced
1 large sweet potato (about 225 g/8 oz), diced
1 x 400 g (14 oz) tin of chopped tomatoes
150 ml (5 fl oz) No Added Salt Vegetable Stock (see page 51)
a pinch of dried oregano
55 g (2 oz) broccoli florets

1. Place the pasta in a pan of water and cook according to the packet instructions.
2. Meanwhile, melt the butter or oil in a pan on a low heat. Add the onions and cook for about five minutes until soft.
3. Add the garlic to the onions and cook for a further 4 minutes.
4. Add the carrots, peppers and sweet potato and cook on low heat for about 6–7 minutes, stirring frequently so they do not burn.
5. Add the tomatoes, stock and oregano. Bring to the boil then reduce the heat and simmer for 15 minutes. Add the broccoli for the final 6 minutes.
6. Drain the pasta and mix in with the sauce and blend to the desired consistency for your baby or, if you are using mini pasta shapes, you can purée the sauce to a smooth purée and pour over the cooked pasta.
7. Serve one portion. Cover and chill the remainder and use within 24 hours or chill then freeze in portions (see page 47).

perfect pasta & scrumptious vegetables

pasta with mushrooms & butter beans

Butter beans are a wonderful ingredient – they provide a creamy texture to purées and act as a natural thickener with a delightful buttery taste.

85 g (3 oz) dried pasta
30 g (1 oz) butter or 1½ tbsp olive oil
55 g (2 oz) onion, finely chopped
85 g (3 oz) leek, sliced
250 g (9 oz) mushrooms, wiped and sliced
200 ml (7 fl oz) No Added Salt Chicken or Vegetable Stock
  (see page 51)
1 tsp freshly chopped parsley or a good pinch of dried parsley
175 g (6 oz) canned butter beans, drained and rinsed

1 Place the pasta in a pan of water and cook according to the packet instructions.

2 Meanwhile, melt the butter or oil in a pan. Add the onions and cook for about five minutes until the onions are soft and transparent. Add the leeks and cook for a further 3–4 minutes.

3 Add the mushrooms and cook for about 6–7 minutes then add the stock, parsley and butter beans. Bring back to the boil then reduce the heat and simmer for about 15 minutes.

4 Drain the pasta. Place it in a blender together with the vegetables and purée to the desired consistency for your baby or, if you are using mini pasta shapes, you can purée the sauce to a smooth purée and pour over the cooked pasta.

5 Serve one portion. Cover and chill the remainder and use within 24 hours or chill then freeze in portions (see page 47).

This recipe has won us two awards – Commended in the Baby Food Soil Association Food Awards in 2004 and Silver in the Taste Of the West Award 2005 in the adult ready-meal category. It's still eaten by our children and remains Callum's favourite. It's easy, quick to make and delicious.

85 g (3 oz) dried pasta
30 g (1 oz) butter or 1½ tbsp olive oil
55 g (2 oz) onion, finely chopped
2–3 carrots (about 300 g/10½ oz in total), thinly sliced
1 × 400 g (14 oz) tin of chopped tomatoes
100 ml (3½ fl oz) No Added Salt Vegetable Stock (see page 51)
1 bay leaf
45 g (1½ oz) mature Cheddar cheese, grated
½ tsp freshly chopped parsley or a pinch of dried parsley

1 Place the pasta in a pan of water and cook according to the packet instructions.
2 Melt the butter or oil and cook the onions for about five minutes until soft. Add the carrots and dried parsley (if using fresh parsley, add at the end) and cook, covered, on a low heat for 10–15 minutes, stirring occasionally.
3 Add the tomatoes, stock and bay leaf, bring to the boil then reduce the heat, cover and simmer for 15 minutes or until the carrots are cooked.
4 Once cooked, remove the bay leaf from the sauce and discard. Add the grated cheese and fresh parsley to the sauce and stir well.
5 Drain the pasta and mix in with the sauce and blend or chop to the desired consistency for your baby or, if you are using mini pasta shapes, you can purée the sauce to a smooth purée and pour over the cooked pasta.
6 Serve one portion. Cover and chill the remainder and use within 24 hours or chill then freeze in portions (see page 47).

perfect pasta & scrumptious vegetables

pasta with sweetcorn, peas & broccoli

makes 4 – 6 portions

A very popular dish, which is colourful and tasty. You can change the combination of vegetables, adding carrots or cauliflower as alternatives. This is a great source of calcium and vitamin C and will be also be enjoyed as your little one gets older.

85 g (3 oz) dried pasta
30 g (1 oz) butter
30 g (1 oz) plain flour
360 ml (12 fl oz) milk
55 g (2 oz) broccoli florets
55 g (2 oz) canned sweetcorn, drained
55 g (2 oz) frozen peas or petit pois
55 g (2 oz) mature Cheddar cheese, grated

1 Place the pasta in a pan of water and cook according to the packet instructions.
2 Melt the butter in a pan on a low heat. Add the flour and stir on a gentle heat. Cook on a low heat for a few minutes until it starts to bubble and resemble honeycomb. Do not overcook at this stage as you will burn the flour.

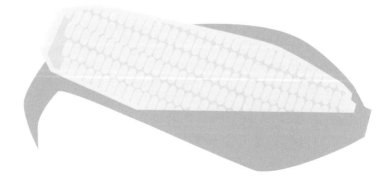

truuuly scrumptious recipes

3 Remove from the heat and gradually add the milk, stirring constantly (you could use a balloon whisk to ensure a smooth sauce).

4 Once all the milk has been added, return the pan to the heat and slowly bring back to the boil, stirring to create a lump-free sauce.

5 Reduce the heat and cook for a few minutes. The sauce will thicken.

6 Remove from the heat and add the grated cheese. Stir until melted.

7 Place the peas and sweetcorn in boiling water and bring to the boil, then add the broccoli. Reduce the heat and simmer for 8–10 minutes until all the vegetables are cooked. Drain.

8 Drain the pasta and add with the cooked vegetables to the cheese sauce. Mix well. Place in a blender and blend or chop to the desired consistency for your baby or, if you are using mini pasta shapes, you can purée the sauce to a smooth purée and pour over the cooked pasta.

9 Serve one portion. Cover and chill the remainder and use within 24 hours or chill then freeze in portions (see page 47).

don't be afraid to use mature Cheddar rather than mild when cooking for your baby – it gives a more cheesy flavour

maisie's macaroni cheese with spinach

makes 5 – 6 portions

This twist to the normal macaroni cheese makes a delicious alternative. The sauce will be a lovely fresh green colour and will be packed full of nutrients such as calcium, vitamin D and iron. Even at the age of six, Maisie still loves this dish and always asks for seconds!

140 g (5 oz) dried macaroni
30 g (1 oz) butter
30 g (1 oz) plain flour
360 ml (12 fl oz) milk
100 g (3½ oz) spinach, washed and tough stalks removed
55 g (2 oz) mature Cheddar cheese, grated

1. Put the macaroni in a pan of boiling water and cook according to the packet instructions.
2. Melt the butter in a pan on a low heat. Add the flour and stir on a gentle heat for a few minutes until it starts to bubble and resemble honeycomb. Do not overcook at this stage as you will burn the flour.
3. Remove from the heat and gradually add the milk, stirring constantly (you could use a balloon whisk to ensure a smooth sauce).
4. Once all the milk has been added return the pan to the heat and slowly bring back to the boil, stirring to create a lump-free sauce.
5. Reduce the heat and cook for a few minutes. The sauce will thicken.
6. Remove from the heat and add the grated cheese. Stir until melted.
7. Steam, microwave or boil the spinach in a little water. Drain well.
8. Drain the pasta and add to the cheese sauce with the spinach, then purée to the desired consistency for your baby or, if you are using mini pasta shapes, you can purée the sauce to a smooth purée and pour over the cooked pasta.
9. Serve one portion. Cover and chill the remainder and use within 24 hours or chill then freeze in portions (see page 47).

 truuuly scrumptious recipes

butternut squash risotto

makes 5 – 6 portions

Butternut squash is a good source of betacarotene. It has a delightful flavour and tastes even better with a little sage. Rice can be introduced to your baby's diet from 6 months. Risottos are a good introduction to rice because Arborio rice needs to be cooked until it is very soft. The dish should be thick and creamy but not too runny – ideal for your baby.

> *30 g (1 oz) butter*
> *55 g (2 oz) onion, finely chopped*
> *1 clove of garlic, crushed*
> *half a large butternut squash or pumpkin (about 500 g/18 oz*
> *   peeled weight), diced*
> *1 tsp freshly chopped sage or a generous pinch of dried sage*
> *115 g (4 oz) Arborio rice*
> *500 ml/17 fl oz No Added Salt Chicken or Vegetable Stock*
> *   (see page 51)*

1 Melt the butter in a pan on a low heat and add the onions. Cook for about five minutes, stirring occasionally until soft and transparent.

2 Add the crushed garlic and cook on a low heat for about 3–4 minutes, stirring occasionally.

3 Add the butternut squash and sage and cook for a further 7–8 minutes then add the rice and cook on a low heat for 6–8 minutes, stirring frequently.

4 Now you need to gradually add the stock. Add about 80–90 ml (3 fl oz) at a time and cook on a low heat, simmering gently and stirring occasionally. Wait for the stock to be absorbed by the rice before you add the next amount. Using this method gives your risotto a really creamy texture and should take around 20–30 minutes to incorporate all the stock.

5 Mash with a fork or purée to the desired consistency for your baby.

6 Serve one portion. Cover and chill the remainder and use within 24 hours or chill then freeze in portions (see page 47).

perfect pasta & scrumptious vegetables

champion chicken, marvellous meat & fantastic fish

Now your baby has moved onto the second stage of weaning it is important to introduce a nutritionally-rich range of foods, including good sources of iron. You should be aiming for three meals a day and introducing foods with more texture. Choose lovely fresh organic meat and fish which often has more flavour and is healthier for your baby. All of our recipes are suitable for babies as they grow into toddlers – we regularly cook dishes for the family from this range, we just omit the puréeing!

chicken & leek risotto

makes 3 – 4 portions

This is a wonderful combination of delicate flavours and makes an excellent comfort food.

30 g (1 oz) butter
55 g (2 oz) onion, finely chopped
55 g (2 oz) leek, sliced
1 skinless, boneless chicken breast (about 125 g/4½ oz), chopped
100 g (3½ oz) Arborio rice
450 ml (15 fl oz) No Added Salt Chicken Stock (see page 51)

1. Melt the butter in a pan on a low heat and add the onions. Cook for about 5 minutes, stirring occasionally until soft and transparent.
2. Add the leeks and cook for a further 3–4 minutes, stirring occasionally.
3. Add the chopped chicken breast to the pan and cook for about 5 minutes, stirring frequently.
4. Add the rice and cook over a low heat for 6–8 minutes, stirring frequently.
5. Now you need to add the stock. Add about 80–90 ml (3 fl oz) at a time and cook on a low heat simmering gently and stirring occasionally. Wait for the stock to be absorbed by the rice before you add the next amount. Using this method gives your risotto a really creamy texture and should take around 20–30 minutes to incorporate all the stock.
6. Chop or purée to the desired consistency for your baby.
7. Serve one portion. Cover and chill the remainder and use within 24 hours or chill then freeze in portions (see page 47).

champion chicken, marvellous meat & fantastic fish

chicken with curly kale & butter beans

This dish is brimming with nutrients. It is packed full of vitamins A, C and E from the vegetables and is a good source of iron, too. The butter beans are a good source of low fat protein and count towards your five portions of fruit and vegetables a day.

30 g (1 oz) butter or 1½ tbsp olive oil
55 g (2 oz) onion, finely chopped
1 skinless, boneless chicken breast (about 150 g/5½ oz), chopped
1 large sweet potato (about 300 g/10½ oz), cubed
2 carrots (about 250 g/9 oz in total), sliced
320 ml (11 fl oz) No Added Salt Chicken Stock (see page 51)
85 g (3 oz) canned butter beans, rinsed and drained
100 g (3½ oz) curly kale, tough stalks removed and finely chopped
a pinch of dried oregano

1   Melt the butter or oil in a pan on a low heat and add the onion. Cook for about 5 minutes until the onions are soft and transparent.

2   Add the diced chicken and cook for about 6 minutes until the chicken is sealed on the outside.

3   Add the sweet potato and carrots and cook for a few minutes, stirring occasionally.

4   Add the stock, butter beans, curly kale and oregano and bring to the boil then reduce the heat, cover and simmer for about 15–20 minutes until the vegetables are soft.

5   Blend to the desired consistency for your baby.

6   Serve one portion. Cover and chill the remainder and use within 24 hours or chill then freeze in portions (see page 47).

truuuly scrumptious recipes

chicken & winter vegetable casserole makes 2 – 3 portions

Much loved by our little ones, this recipe has been well used. It's a simple combination which delivers on taste and health. Eat a big bowl of it yourself and it will leave you feeling healthily satisfied.

15 g (½ oz) butter or 2 tsp olive oil
30 g (1 oz) onion, finely chopped
20 g (¾ oz) leek, finely sliced
1 skinless, boneless chicken breast or 2 large thighs skinned and boned (about 140 g/5 oz), chopped into small pieces
1 potato (about 175 g/6 oz), diced
1 carrot (about 85 g/3 oz), thinly sliced
220 ml (7 fl oz) No Added Salt Chicken Stock (see page 51)
55 g (2 oz) broccoli florets

1. Melt the butter or oil in a pan on a low heat and add the onion. Cook on a low heat for about 3–4 minutes. Add the leek and cook for a further 2 minutes.

2. Add the chicken and cook on a low heat for 4 minutes. Add the potato and carrot and cook for a further 10 minutes, stirring occasionally.

3. Add the stock and broccoli. Bring to the boil, cover and simmer, stirring occasionally until the potatoes are cooked (about 15–20 minutes).

4. Remove from the heat and purée to the desired consistency for your baby.

5. Serve one portion. Cover and chill the remainder and use within 24 hours or freeze in portions (see page 47).

creamy chicken & vegetables with sweet potato mash

makes 5 – 6 portions

This is an ideal way of using some cooked chicken. Keep some succulent chicken back from a roast but don't forget not to add salt if you are planning to use some meat for your baby. You could substitute the sweet potato mash with pasta as a variation.

30 g (1 oz) butter
30 g (1 oz) plain flour
360 ml (12 fl oz) milk
75 g (2½ oz) broccoli florets
75 g (2½ oz) frozen or canned sweetcorn
1 skinless, boneless chicken breast (about 125 g/4½ oz
*   uncooked weight) or cooked chicken (about 85g /3 oz),*
*   chopped*

For the mash:
30 g (1 oz) butter
60 ml (2 fl oz) milk
1 large potato (about 250 g/9 oz), diced
1 sweet potato (about 200 g/7 oz), diced

1   Preheat the oven to 180°C/350°F/gas mark 4.
2   If you are using uncooked chicken, place the chicken in a suitable dish and bake in the oven for about 25 minutes until cooked.
3   For the mash, place the potatoes and sweet potatoes in a pan and cover with cold water. Bring to the boil then reduce the heat and simmer for about 15 minutes until cooked.

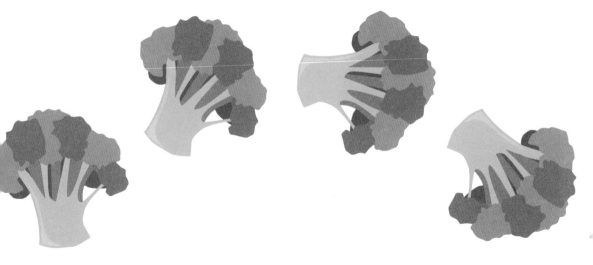

4 Meanwhile, put the broccoli and sweetcorn into a pan and cover with boiling water. Bring back to the boil then reduce the heat and simmer for 10 minutes until cooked. Drain.

5 While the vegetables are cooking, melt the butter over a low heat and add the flour and stir on a gentle heat. Cook on a low heat for a few minutes until it starts to bubble and resemble honeycomb. Do not overcook at this stage as you will burn the flour.

6 Remove from the heat and gradually add the milk, stirring constantly (you could use a balloon whisk to ensure a smooth sauce).

7 Once all the milk has been incorporated, return the pan to the heat and slowly bring back to the boil, stirring to create a lump-free sauce.

8 Reduce the heat and cook for a few minutes. The sauce will thicken. Remove the sauce from the heat.

9 Remove the chicken from the oven and chop into small pieces. Add to the sauce along with the broccoli and sweetcorn.

10 Drain the potatoes when cooked. Place back in the pan and add the butter and milk and mash.

11 Chop or blend the creamy chicken and vegetable sauce to the desired consistency for your baby and stir in the sweet potato mash.

12 Serve one portion. Cover and chill the remainder and use within 24 hours or chill then freeze in portions (see page 47).

tasty turkey casserole makes 6 – 7 portions

We often only think of buying sprouts at Christmas, however, they have one of the highest levels of vitamin C of any vegetable and are very nutritious. This combination of ingredients makes a really flavoursome dish, which you could serve to your baby on Christmas day!

1 carrot(about 150 g/5 oz), sliced
100 g (3½ oz) brussel sprouts, halved
1 large potato (about 250 g/8½ oz), diced
1 sweet potato (about 175 g/6 oz), diced
200 g (7 oz) turkey breasts or sliced turkey, cut into strips
50 ml (15 fl oz) No Added Salt Chicken Stock (see page 51)
55 g (2 oz) broccoli florets
1 tsp freshly chopped sage or ½ tsp dried sage

1 Put the carrots, sprouts, potato, sweet potato, turkey, sage and the stock into a pan and bring to the boil. Reduce the heat and simmer for 15 minutes, stirring occasionally.

2 Add the broccoli and cook for a further 5–7 minutes until all the vegetables are cooked.

3 Remove from the heat and blend to the desired consistency for your baby.

4 Serve one portion. Cover and chill the remainder and use within 24 hours or chill then freeze in portions (see page 47)

truuuly scrumptious recipes

fisherman's medley

makes 6 – 7 portions

This recipe isn't too fishy and blends well with the sweet root vegetables.

1 sweet potato (about 250 g/8 oz), diced
2 carrots (about 250 g/8 oz in total), thinly sliced
1 courgette (about 200 g/7 oz), sliced
250 g (8 oz) cod, salmon or trout, with skin on
200 ml (7 fl oz) milk
3 peppercorns
1 bay leaf
30 g (1 oz) butter
75 g (2½ oz) onion, finely chopped
200 g (7 oz) tinned chopped tomatoes
1 tbsp freshly chopped parsley

1. Place the sweet potato and carrots in a pan and cover with boiling water. Bring to the boil then reduce the heat and simmer for about 15 minutes.

2. Add the courgette and cook for 5 minutes. Drain. Alternatively, place the vegetables in a steamer and steam in the same order until cooked.

3. Put the fish in a pan with the milk, peppercorns and bay leaf. Bring to the boil then reduce the heat and simmer gently for about 10 minutes until the fish starts to flake and is cooked through. Strain the milk and put to one side and discard the bay leaf and peppercorns. Once the fish has cooled slightly you will need to remove the skin and break up and flake the flesh to remove any bones and loose scales.

4. Meanwhile melt the butter and cook the onions for 5 minutes until soft, stirring occasionally.

5. Add the tomatoes and parsley . Cook for 5 minutes on a low heat.

6. Finally add the cooked vegetables, fish and reserved milk to the tomato mix. Stir well. Purée or chop to the desired consistency for your baby.

7. Serve one portion. Cover and chill the remainder and use within 24 hours or chill then freeze in portions (see page 47).

salmon & broccoli pie

This delicious recipe is a real winner – it won the Soil Association Organic Baby Food Award in 2002 and received Commended in the Adult Prepared Food Dishes in 2004. It seems to be popular with everyone, maybe because it has a subtle fish flavour from the salmon which is complemented by the creamy sauce and mash, it makes it very moreish!

1 salmon fillet (about 155 g/ 5½ oz)
360 ml (12 fl oz) milk
30 g (1 oz) butter
30 g (1 oz) plain flour
55 g (2 oz) broccoli florets
55 g (2 oz) mature Cheddar cheese, grated

For the mash:-
30 g (1 oz) butter
60 ml (2 fl oz) milk
2 potatoes (about 425 g/15 oz in total), diced

1. Place the salmon fillet in a pan and cover with the milk. Bring to the boil then reduce the heat and simmer for 10–15 minutes until the salmon starts to flake and is cooked through.
2. Drain the salmon and set aside, reserving the milk to make the cheese sauce.
3. Once the salmon is cooled you will need to remove the skin and break up and flake the salmon to look for and remove any bones.
4. To make the mash, rinse the potatoes with cold water to remove any starch. Add to a pan of boiling water and cook for 15–20 minutes until tender.
5. Drain the potatoes once cooked. Place back in the pan and add the butter and milk. Mash until smooth.

truuuly scrumptious recipes

6   While the potatoes are cooking you can make the cheese sauce. Melt the butter in a pan on a low heat. Add the flour and cook on a low heat for a few minutes until it starts to bubble and resemble honeycomb. Do not overcook at this stage as you will burn the flour.

7   Remove from the heat and gradually add the reserved milk, stirring constantly (you could use a balloon whisk to ensure a smooth sauce).

8   Once all the milk has been incorporated, return the pan to the heat and slowly bring back to the boil, stirring to create a lump-free sauce.

9   Reduce the heat and cook for a few minutes. The sauce will thicken. Remove from the heat and add the grated cheese. Stir until melted.

10 Put the broccoli in a pan and add enough boiling water to cover. Bring to the boil then reduce the heat and simmer for about 8–10 minutes until cooked. Alternatively, steam until cooked.

11 Add the cooked broccoli and flaked salmon to the cheese sauce. Stir well. You can then either stir in the mashed potato and serve or place all the ingredients in a blender and blend to the desired consistency.

12 Serve one portion. Cover and chill the remainder and use within 24 hours or chill then freeze in portions (see page 47)

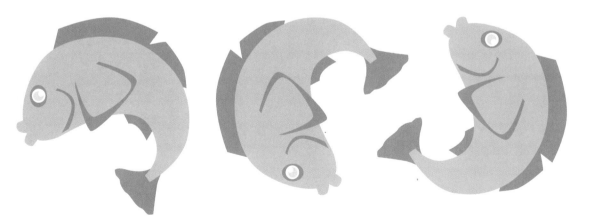

champion chicken, marvellous meat & fantastic fish

tuna pasta bake

Tuna is a good source of protein and, of course, omega-3. Fresh tuna steak is widely available and delicious but this dish will be just as successful with canned tuna. Choose canned tuna in water or oil as the salt content is much higher in brine. It is ideal for toddlers and older children who can choose which kind of pasta to use. This is still a real favourite of Maisie's, who is now seven.

1 fresh tuna steak (about 125 g/4½ oz), or canned tuna chunks
360 ml (12 fl oz) milk
half a bay leaf
45 g (1½ oz) peas, frozen
55 g (2 oz) sweetcorn, canned
100 g (3½ oz) dried pasta
30 g (1 oz) butter
30 g (1 oz) plain flour
45 g (1½ oz) mature Cheddar cheese, grated

1. If using fresh tuna place the tuna in a pan and cover with the milk. Add the bay leaf. Bring to the boil then reduce the heat and simmer for 10–15 minutes until the tuna steak starts to flake and is cooked through. If you are using canned tuna drain and set aside to add to the sauce once cooked.

2. Drain the tuna and set aside, reserving the milk to make the cheese sauce. Discard the bay leaf.

3. Put the pasta in a pan of boiling water and cook according to the packet instructions.

4. Place the peas and sweetcorn in a pan of boiling water and cook for 5–7 minutes.

5. Melt the butter in a pan on a low heat. Add the flour and cook on a low heat for a few minutes until it starts to bubble and resemble honeycomb. Do not overcook at this stage as you will burn the flour.

 truuuly scrumptious recipes

if you are cooking your vegetables in butter, you can mix in a bit of olive oil – this will stop the butter from burning

6 Remove from the heat and gradually add the reserved milk, stirring constantly (you could use a balloon whisk to ensure a smooth sauce).

7 Once all the milk has been incorporated, return the pan to the heat and slowly bring back to the boil, stirring to create a lump-free sauce.

8 Reduce the heat and cook for a few minutes. The sauce will thicken.

9 Remove from the heat and add the grated cheese and stir until melted. Add the peas, sweetcorn and tuna and cooked pasta and stir through. Either purée to the desired consistency for your baby or, if you are using mini pasta shapes, you can purée the sauce to a smooth purée and pour over the cooked pasta.

10 Serve one portion. Cover and chill the remainder and use within 24 hours or chill then freeze in portions (see page 47).

italian style tuna with pasta

makes 5 – 6 portions

This dish has a wonderful appearance with a medley of colours from the vegetables. Choosing vegetables which are all different colours will mean you are including a good range of vital nutrients. If you use oil instead of butter and leave out the cheese, you have an excellent meal for those choosing dairy-free recipes.

30 g (1 oz) butter or 1½ tbsp olive oil
55 g (2 oz) onion, finely chopped
1 carrot (about 170 g/6 oz)
half a yellow pepper, (about 100 g/3½ oz), deseeded and diced
half a large courgette (about 110 g/4 oz), sliced
1 × 400 g (14 oz) tin of chopped tomatoes
1 × 200 g (7 oz) tin of tuna in spring water
85 g (3 oz) dried pasta
Cheddar cheese, grated (optional)

1 Put the pasta in a pan of boiling water and cook according to the packet instructions.
2 Heat the butter or oil in a pan then add the onion and cook for about 5 minutes, stirring occasionally, until the onions are soft and transparent.

truuuly scrumptious recipes

3 Add the carrots and cook for 6 minutes, stirring occasionally.

4 Add the pepper and courgette and cook for a further 5 minutes on a low heat, stirring occasionally, then add the tomatoes. Bring to the boil and simmer for about 15 minutes.

5 Drain the tuna and add to the sauce, stir and cook for a further 2–3 minutes.

6 Drain the pasta and stir into the sauce, with some grated cheese, if using. Chop or blend to the desired consistency for your baby or, if you are using mini pasta shapes, you can purée the sauce to a smooth purée and pour over the cooked pasta.

7 Serve one portion. Cover and chill the remainder and use within 24 hours or chill then freeze in portions (see page 47).

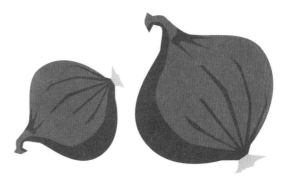

jack's cottage pie

makes 6 – 7 portions

This is an all-time favourite of all our children, particularly Jack who can't get enough of anything accompanied by fluffy mashed potatoes.

> *30 g (1 oz) butter or 1½ tbsp olive oil*
> *55 g (2 oz) onion, finely chopped*
> *1 carrot (about 150 g/5 oz), sliced*
> *250 g (9 oz) extra lean beef steak mince*
> *55 g (2 oz) mushrooms, sliced*
> *85 g (3 oz) tinned chopped tomatoes or passata*
> *180 ml (6½ fl oz) No Added Salt Beef or Chicken Stock*
>   *(see page 51)*
> *½ tsp low salt yeast extract*
>
> *For the mash:*
> *2 potatoes (about 450 g/1 lb), diced*
> *30 g (1 oz) butter*
> *60 ml (2 fl oz) milk*

1 Heat the butter or oil on a low heat and add the onions. Cook for about 5 minutes until soft and transparent.
2 Add the carrots to the onion and cook, covered, for 6 minutes on a low-medium heat, stirring occasionally.
3 Add the mince and cook until browned all over, stirring throughout to ensure even cooking.
4 Add the mushrooms and cook for a further 5 minutes.
5 Add the tomatoes, stock and low-salt yeast extract. Bring back to the boil then reduce the heat and simmer gently for 15 minutes.

6   Meanwhile, rinse the diced potatoes with cold water to remove starch. Add to a separate pan of boiling water and cook for 15–20 minutes until tender.

7   Drain the potatoes. Place back in the pan and add the butter and milk. Mash until smooth. Remove the mince from the heat. You can either blend the meat on its own and then stir into the mash or you can mix the meat into the mash and blend together to the desired consistency for your baby.

8   Serve one portion. Cover and chill the remainder and use within 24 hours or chill then freeze in portions (see page 47).

if you whisk your potatoes after mashing them you'll create an even fluffier texture!

spaghetti bolognese

This dish is always popular and one you could be making for many years. If your baby is eating lumps well you could cut this recipe up with a knife and fork after it is cooked rather than puréeing. Try different pasta shapes like shells or twists; it doesn't have to be spaghetti. Our children like to sprinkle cheese on top.

30 g (1 oz) butter or 1½ tbsp olive oil
55 g (2 oz) onion, finely chopped
1 clove of garlic, crushed
250 g (9 oz) extra lean beef steak mince
100 g (3½ oz) mushrooms, sliced
1½ tins of chopped tomatoes (600 g/21 oz)
1 bay leaf
½ tsp dried mixed herbs
85 g (3 oz) dried spaghetti or other pasta shapes

1 Put the pasta in a pan of boiling water and cook according to the packet instructions.

2 Heat the butter or oil in a pan on a low heat. Add the onions and cook on a low heat for about 5 minutes until soft, stirring occasionally.

3 Add the crushed garlic and cook for a further 3–4 minutes, then add the beef mince and cook on medium heat for about 5–7 minutes, stirring frequently until all the meat is browned. Add the mushrooms and cook for 5–6 minutes.

4 Finally add the tomatoes, bay leaf and mixed herbs. Bring to the boil, then reduce the heat and simmer for 20 minutes, stirring occasionally.

5 Remove the bay leaf from the sauce then add the cooked spaghetti or other pasta shapes. Place in a blender and purée to the desired consistency for your baby or, if you are using mini pasta shapes, you can purée the sauce to a smooth purée and pour over the cooked pasta.

6 Serve one portion. Cover and chill the remainder and use within 24 hours or chill then freeze in portions (see page 47).

beef stew

Fill your kitchen with the delicious aromas of this home-cooked stew. Stews are really very easy to make and can be left simmering away in the oven. The long cooking time helps tenderise the meat and develop the flavours. This is really no different to an adult recipe – except for the addition of a glug of red wine in the adult version!

>30 g (1 oz) butter or 1½ tbsp olive oil
>55 g (2 oz) onion, finely chopped
>1 clove of garlic, crushed
>400 g (14 oz) stewing beef, cubed
>1 tsp freshly chopped sage or ½ tsp dried sage
>2 carrots (about 200 g/7 oz in total), sliced
>1 large potato (about 320 g/11 oz), diced
>1 small parsnip (about 150 g/5 oz) or butternut squash, diced
>200 g (7 oz) tinned chopped tomatoes or passata
>360 ml (12 fl oz) No Added Salt Chicken Stock (see page 51)
>1 bay leaf

1 Preheat the oven to 160°C/325°F/gas mark 3.
2 Heat the butter or oil in a flameproof casserole dish. Add the onions and cook for about 5 minutes until soft. Add the crushed garlic and cook for a further 3–4 minutes.
3 Add the beef and sage and stir until browned over a medium heat. Then add the carrots, potato, parsnip or butternut squash, tomatoes, stock and bay leaf and bring back to the boil. Remove from the heat.
4 Place the lid on the casserole dish and place in the oven and cook until the meat is very tender (about 2–2½ hours).
5 Remove the bay leaf and either mash the casserole with a fork or purée to the desired consistency.
6 Serve one portion. Cover and chill the remainder and use within 24 hours or chill then freeze in portions (see page 47).

shepherd's pie
makes 6 – 7 portions

Babies enjoy the texture of mashed potato. By combining it with the meat base you are introducing small soft lumps and adding more flavour.

We often get asked whether Shepherd's Pie is made with beef or lamb mince, so to clarify; Shepherd's Pie is traditionally made with lamb, Cottage Pie is made with beef. Lamb mince is widely available and is an excellent source of protein and iron. Choose Maris Piper potatoes – they will create a lovely light and fluffy mash.

30 g (1 oz) butter or 1½ tbsp olive oil
55 g (2 oz) onion, finely chopped
1 carrot (about 150 g/5 oz), sliced
250 g (9 oz) extra lean lamb mince
85 g (3 oz) tinned chopped tomatoes or passata
55 g (2 oz) frozen peas
180 ml (6½ fl oz) No Added Salt Chicken Stock (see page 51)
½ tsp dried marjoram

For the mash:
2 potatoes (about 430 g/14 oz in total), diced
30 g (1 oz) butter
60 ml (2 fl oz) milk

1 Heat the butter or oil in a pan on a low heat and add the onions. Cook for about 5 minutes until soft and transparent.

2 Add the carrots to the onion and cook, covered, for 6 minutes on a low heat, stirring occasionally.

3 Add the mince and cook until browned all over, stirring throughout to ensure even cooking – this will take about 8–10 minutes.

4 Add the tomatoes, peas, stock and marjoram and bring back to the boil then reduce the heat and simmer gently for 15 minutes.

5 Meanwhile, rinse the diced potatoes in cold water to remove the starch. Place in a separate pan and cover with boiling water. Bring back to the boil and cook for 15–20 minutes until tender.

truuuly scrumptious recipes

6   Drain the potatoes then put back in the saucepan, add the butter and milk and mash until smooth.

7   Remove the mince sauce from the heat. You can either blend the meat on its own and then stir into the mash or you can mix the meat into the mash and blend together to the desired consistency for your baby.

8   Serve one portion. Cover and chill the remainder and use within 24 hours or chill then freeze in portions (see page 47).

lamb & apricot casserole makes 6–7 portions

The sweet flavour from the apricots works well combined with the other savoury ingredients in this recipe. Remember to use organic apricots which will be darker in colour and do not contain sulphur dioxide. The sweetness is not overpowering and is subtle and delicious. It could be served on its own or with some rice or mashed potato. Topsy often cooks it for friends who come round for supper.

30 g (1 oz) butter or 1½ tbsp olive oil
55 g (2 oz) onion, finely chopped
340 g (12 oz) stewing lamb, cubed
a pinch of dried thyme and a pinch of dried rosemary
1 carrot (about 200 g/7 oz), sliced
1 sweet potato (about 225 g/8 oz), diced
200 g (7 oz) tinned chopped tomatoes
30 g (1 oz) soft and ready to eat organic apricots, rinsed and chopped
250 ml (8½ fl oz) No Added Salt Chicken Stock (see page 51)
85 g (3 oz) curly kale, tough stalks removed and chopped

continued from page 113

1 Preheat the oven to 150°C/300°F/gas mark 2.

2 Heat the butter or oil in an oven- and hob-proof casserole dish. Add the onions and cook for about 5 minutes, stirring frequently, until the onions are soft and transparent.

3 Add the lamb and herbs and brown the meat, stirring frequently. Then add the carrot, sweet potato, tinned tomatoes, chopped apricots and stock. Bring back to the boil and take off the heat.

4 Put the lid on and then transfer the dish to the centre of the oven and cook for 2–2½ hours until the meat is very tender.

5 Add the curly kale half an hour before the end of the cooking time and stir in.

6 Chop or purée to the desired consistency for your baby.

7 Serve one portion. Cover and chill the remainder and use within 24 hours or chill then freeze in portions (see page 47).

truuuly scrumptious recipes

chicken liver with root vegetables

makes 5 – 6 portions

Unfortunately most people have bad memories of liver. However, cooked in the right way, with a lovely selection of root vegetables, it really is worth revisiting. Chicken livers are tender with a delicate, mild flavour – they are also an excellent source of vitamin A and iron.

30 g (1 oz) butter or 1½ tbsp olive oil
55 g (2 oz) onion, finely chopped
75 g (2½ oz) leek, sliced
2 medium carrots (about 225 g/8 oz in total), sliced
115 g (4 oz) chicken liver, chopped
1 sweet potato (about 250 g/8½ oz), diced
1 potato (about 250 g/8½ oz), diced
320 ml (11 fl oz) No Added Salt Chicken Stock (see page 51)

1 Heat the butter or oil in a pan on a low heat and add the onions. Cook for about 5 minutes on a low heat, stirring frequently until the onions are soft.

2 Add the leeks and cook for about 3–4 minutes, stirring occasionally. Then add the carrots and cook, covered, on a low heat, stirring occasionally for about 7 minutes.

3 Add the chopped chicken liver and cook on a low heat for about 8–10 minutes, stirring occasionally.

4 Finally add the sweet potato, potato and the stock and bring to the boil. Reduce the heat and simmer for 10–15 minutes, stirring occasionally, until the potatoes are cooked.

5 Remove from the heat and blend to the desired consistency for your baby.

6 Serve one portion. Cover and chill the remainder and use within 24 hours or chill then freeze in portions (see page 47).

champion chicken, marvellous meat & fantastic fish

brilliant breakfasts & perfect puddings

At stage two of weaning your baby will begin to enjoy the social aspect of eating with the rest of the family. By participating and observing at mealtimes, he'll be learning important social skills, as well as appreciating the satisfaction of sharing and enjoying food. Your baby will be growing quite quickly now and you will find his appetite increasing as well. He may enjoy fruit or dairy desserts after his savoury food so we have included some delicious fruit combinations in the following recipes. There are also two rice pudding recipes – a nursery staple – one made with coconut milk for a dairy-free option. Both are made without sugar and are extremely creamy and delicious.

apple & raisin porridge

Porridge is a great start to the day, full of complex carbohydrates which release energy slowly. Teamed with luscious apples and raisins this recipe is naturally sweet and it may prove hard to resist helping yourself to a spoonful or two.

2 apples (about 250 g/9 oz in total), peeled, cored and sliced
60 ml (2 fl oz) water
15 g (½ oz) raisins
a pinch of cinnamon
75 g (2½ oz) porridge oats
360 ml (12 fl oz) milk

1. Place the apples in a pan with the water, raisins and cinnamon. Bring to the boil then reduce the heat and simmer for 10–15 minutes until the apples are soft.
2. Meanwhile, place the oats and milk in a separate saucepan and bring to the boil. Reduce the heat and simmer gently until cooked.
3. Purée the apples and raisins and stir into the cooked porridge.
4. Serve one portion. Cover and chill the remainder and use within 24 hours or chill then freeze in portions (see page 47).

brilliant breakfasts & perfect puddings

banana porridge
makes 3 – 4 portions

This recipe is one of our favourites. When you taste it you won't believe it doesn't contain any sugar or cream. Although many of us don't like eating over-ripe bananas by themselves they are perfect for this recipe. We make big batches of this so there is enough for the whole family!

75 g (2½ oz) porridge oats
360 ml (12 fl oz) milk
1 medium ripe banana (about 115 g/4 oz)

1 Put the oats and milk into a saucepan and bring slowly to the boil. Reduce the heat and simmer gently until the oats are cooked.

2 Meanwhile, mash the banana with a fork or purée with a hand-held blender.

3 Once the oats are cooked, remove from the heat and stir in the banana.

4 Cool to the correct temperature before serving to your baby (you can add a little cold milk to help it cool quickly). Cover and chill the remainder in the fridge and use within 24 hours or freeze in portions (see page 47).

 truuuly scrumptious recipes

apples & prunes

makes 4 – 5 portions

If your baby has been suffering with constipation this is a great natural remedy as the prunes are full of fibre. Prunes are naturally sweet and complement the apple purée perfectly.

> *6 apples (about 800 g/1¾ lb in total), peeled, cored and sliced*
> *12 prunes (about 85 g/3 oz in total), stoned*
> *60 ml (2 fl oz) water*

1. Place the apples in a pan and just cover with boiling water. Bring to the boil then reduce the heat and simmer for about 10 minutes until cooked. Alternatively, steam the apples until tender – about 10 minutes.

2. Place the prunes in a pan and add the water. Bring to the boil then reduce the heat and simmer for about 7–8 minutes until the water has been absorbed.

3. Put the prunes and apples into a blender and blend to a smooth purée.

4. Serve one portion. Cover and chill the remainder and use within 24 hours or chill then freeze in portions (see page 47).

apple, pear & kiwi makes 3 – 4 portions

This is a big favourite with our children, even now. Don't worry about the kiwi seeds in the puree, they are soft and perfectly safe to eat. However, they are not digested and will be visible in nappies!

> *3 apples (about 400 g/14 oz in total), peeled, cored and sliced*
> *1 pear (about 170 g/6 oz), peeled, cored and sliced*
> *1 kiwi fruit (about 85 g/3 oz), peeled and rinsed*

1 Place the apples in a pan and add enough boiling water to cover the fruit and bring to the boil. Reduce the heat and simmer for about 5 minutes.

2 Add the pears and simmer for a further 5 minutes until all the fruit is soft. Drain. Alternatively, steam the fruit in the same order until soft.

3 Add the cooked apple and pear to a blender with the kiwi and blend to a smooth purée.

4 Serve one portion. Cover and chill the remainder and use within 24 hours or chill then freeze in portions (see page 47).

If you have an over-ripe banana in your fruit bowl don't throw it away – they are naturally sweeter and give a better flavour to this purée, which is also delicious when eaten with natural yoghurt. This recipe has won two awards: runner-up in the Dried Fruit Awards and silver in Taste of the West in 2005. Remember to use organic apricots which will be darker in colour and do not contain sulphur dioxide. Due to the organic apricots, this recipe produces a dark almost syrupy purée.

> *2 pears (about 340 g/12 oz in total), peeled, cored and sliced*
> *1 banana (about 125 g/4½ oz), sliced*
> *30 g (1 oz) soft and ready to eat organic apricots, rinsed*
> *60 ml (2 fl oz) boiling water*

1. Place the pears in a pan and add enough boiling water just to cover the fruit. Bring to the boil then simmer for about 5–10 minutes until the pear is soft. Drain. Alternatively, steam the pear for about 5–10 minutes until soft.

2. Meanwhile, place the apricots in a pan and cover with the water. Simmer for about 5 minutes until the water is absorbed and the apricots are re-hydrated.

3. Place the cooked pears and apricots together with the banana in a blender and blend to a smooth purée.

4. Serve one portion. Cover and chill the remainder and use within 24 hours or chill then freeze in portions (see page 47).

brilliant breakfasts & perfect puddings

seasonal fruit compote makes 4 ~ 5 portions

This compote is really at its best made with seasonal fruit – juicy plums, nectarines and peaches make this a perfect summer treat. You can change the combination according to the season so that it always tastes fresh and juicy and bursts with flavour – as well as vitamin C.

3 apples (about 400 g/14 oz in total), peeled, cored and sliced
1 ripe banana (about 160 g/5½ oz), sliced
1 pear (about 170 g/6 oz), peeled, cored and sliced
1 peach, nectarine or plum (140 g/5 oz), peeled and sliced
1 kiwi fruit (about 85 g/3 oz), peeled and sliced
1 orange, freshly squeezed (optional)

1 Place the apples in a pan with just enough boiling water to cover the fruit. Bring to the boil then reduce the heat and simmer for 10 minutes until soft. Alternatively, steam for 10 minutes until soft.

2 Place all the remaining fruit, cooked apple and freshly squeezed orange juice in a blender and purée.

3 Serve one portion. Cover and chill the remainder and use within 24 hours or chill then freeze in portions (see page 47).

truuuly scrumptious recipes

apple & mango
makes 3 – 4 portions

This is the perfect opportunity to introduce a little tropical flavour – and you can always enjoy the spare half yourself. This product won us a silver award in the Taste of the West Awards (judged against adult desserts) in 2005.

3 apples (about 400 g/14 oz in total) peeled, cored and sliced
half a ripe mango, diced

1 Place the apples in a pan with just enough boiling water to cover the fruit. Bring to the boil then reduce the heat and simmer for about 10 minutes until soft. Alternatively, steam the apples for about 10 minutes until soft.

2 Place the cooked apples in a blender with the chopped mango. Purée to the desired consistency for your baby.

3 Serve one portion. Cover and chill the remainder and use within 24 hours or chill then freeze in portions (see page 47).

apples, blueberries & quinoa
makes 3 – 4 portions

Blueberries are a top superfood to feed your baby – bursting with antioxidants and flavour. The addition of quinoa to this deep purple purée gives it a thicker texture and is ideal when your baby is ready to try move on to the second stage of weaning.

4 sweet apples (about 450 g/1 lb in total), peeled, cored and sliced
85 g (3 oz) blueberries
250 ml (8½ fl oz) boiling water
2 heaped dessert spoons flaked quinoa

continued from page 123

1 Place the apples and blueberries in a saucepan and cover with the boiling water. Bring to the boil then reduce the heat, cover and simmer for 5 minutes.

2 Add the quinoa and simmer for a further 10–15 minutes until the apples are cooked and the quinoa is absorbed. Stir frequently.

3 Place the contents of the pan into a blender and purée to the desired consistency. To thin the purée if necessary, add more boiled water.

4 Serve one portion. Cover and chill the remainder and use within 24 hours or chill then freeze in portions (see page 47).

dried fruit compote makes 3 – 4 portions

Often people have a negative view of prunes – we want to change this. As well as a good source of fibre, dried fruit is an excellent source of iron and, combined with the apple and pears which provide vitamin C, it will be more easily absorbed. This recipe really does taste delicious and you will be pleasantly surprised!

3 apples (about 400 g/14 oz in total), peeled, cored and sliced
2 pears (about 300 g/10½ oz in total), peeled, cored and sliced
4 soft and ready to eat figs (about 55 g/2 oz)
5 soft and ready to eat prunes (about 30 g/1 oz), stoned
100 ml (3½ fl oz) boiling water
¼ tsp ground cinnamon

truuuly scrumptious recipes

1. Place the apples in a pan and cover with water. Bring to the boil then reduce the heat and simmer for 5 minutes. Add the pear and simmer for a further 5 minutes. Drain. Alternatively, steam the fruit in the same order until soft.

2. Place the dried fruit in a small pan and add the boiled water. Bring back to the boil then reduce heat and simmer gently for about 10 minutes until the water has been absorbed by the fruit.

3. Once all the fruit is cooked, add the cinnamon. Either place in a blender and purée then press through a sieve to remove the crunchy fig seeds, or place immediately through the fine sieve on a mouli to remove the seeds.

4. Serve one portion. Cover and chill the remainder and use within 24 hours or chill then freeze in portions (see page 47).

dried fruit is a good, natural remedy if your baby is suffering from constipation

brilliant breakfasts & perfect puddings

coconut rice pudding makes 2 – 3 portions

Rice pudding is a nursery classic but the use of coconut milk gives this a yummy twist that also makes it a great one to try if your baby can't have milk or dairy products. We were prompted to try it because we've had so many requests for dairy-free desserts.

1 x 400 ml (14 oz) can coconut milk
55 g (2 oz) pudding rice
¼ tsp vanilla extract

1. Preheat the oven to 150°C/300°F/gas mark 2.
2. Pour the coconut milk into a jug and whisk to combine as it will have separated in the can.
3. Add the coconut milk to an ovenproof pudding dish. Then add the pudding rice and vanilla extract and stir.
4. Cook in the oven for 1½ hours until the rice pudding is rich and creamy. Stir every half an hour.
5. You can serve this on its own or mix with some puréed fruit. Serve one portion. Cover and chill the remainder and use within 24 hours or chill then freeze in portions (see page 47).

archie's rice pudding

makes 3 – 4 portions

Rice pudding should be creamy, comforting and moreish – and this is no exception! As the dish cooks the milk naturally becomes creamier and its natural sugars caramelise. Personally, we would double the recipe and eat the extra ourselves. Archie could eat it until the cows come home!

460 ml (16 fl oz) milk
55 g (2 oz) pudding rice
¼ tsp vanilla extract
a knob of butter, plus extra for greasing

1. Preheat the oven to 150°C/300°F/Gas Mark 2. Grease an ovenproof dish with butter.
2. Add the milk, pudding rice and vanilla extract to the buttered dish and stir.
3. Chop the butter into small pieces and dot on the surface of the milk.
4. Cook in the over for 2–2½ hours until the rice pudding is rich and creamy. Stir every half an hour. It will form a skin which you can either take off (and eat separately!) or stir in. You can serve this on its own or mix with some puréed fruit.
5. Serve one portion. Cover and chill the remainder and use within 24 hours or chill then freeze in portions (see page 47).

semolina with pear & apricots

makes 3 – 4 portions

If you feel limited to just yoghurts as a dairy dessert then try this. When cooked properly, semolina gives a delicious creamy texture that looks a little like custard when combined with pears and apricots. Remember to use organic apricots which will be darker in colour and do not contain sulphur dioxide.

> *4 soft and ready to eat organic apricots (about 30 g/1 oz), rinsed*
> *60 ml (2 fl oz) boiling water*
> *360 ml (12 fl oz) milk*
> *45 g (1½ oz) semolina*
> *1 pear (about 125 g/4½ oz), peeled, cored and sliced*

1. Place the apricots in a pan and add the boiled water. Bring to the boil then reduce heat and simmer gently for 6–8 minutes to re-hydrate the apricots. Remove from the heat.
2. Put the milk and the semolina in a small pan and bring to the boil. Reduce the heat and simmer for about 10 minutes, stirring occasionally.
3. Meanwhile, place the pear in a blender with the apricots and blend. Mix this fruit purée into the semolina and serve.
4. Serve one portion. Cover and chill the remainder and use within 24 hours or chill then freeze in portions (see page 47).

truuuly scrumptious recipes

yoghurt & dried fruit

makes 2 portions

Natural yoghurt is good base for combining with any of the fruit purées from both the first and second stage recipes. Put a portion in a lidded pot and you have a quick, portable dessert full of home-made goodness!

> *100 g (3½ oz) Dried Fruit Compote (see page 124)*
> *100 g (3½ oz) natural yoghurt*

1. Stir the fruit compote into the natural yoghurt and mix well.
2. Serve one portion. Keep the remainder chilled and use within 48 hours.

yoghurt & mixed berries

makes 2 – 3 portions

By itself the yoghurt can be sharp but don't forget your baby won't be used to sugary sweet foods. The natural sweetness from the berries is just enough to balance the flavour from the yoghurt – and they make a lovely colour when puréed together.

> *200 g (7 oz) natural yoghurt*
> *45 g (1½ oz) strawberries*
> *30 g (1 oz) raspberries*
> *45 g (1½ oz) blueberries*

1. Place the yoghurt and berries in a blender and purée to a smooth consistency.
2. Serve one portion and reserve the remainder in the fridge and use within 24 hours.

brilliant breakfasts & perfect puddings

fabulous finger foods

By the age of about nine months your baby may have acquired some teeth and will be growing rapidly. Even if his pearly whites haven't made an appearance, don't think this means your baby can't have finger foods; babies have very strong gums! Finger foods are ideal for giving him some independence – he can use his hands to feed himself and practice chewing – and also help to comfort sore gums. You can offer a variety of finger foods from ripe chopped fruit, toast fingers, slices of cheese to any of the recipes from this section. Remember, never leave your baby unsupervised when eating in case of choking.

steamed vegetables

Try not to over- or undercook the vegetables: if they are too mushy they will be difficult to hold; if they are undercooked they will be difficult to swallow.

half a medium carrot, cut into sticks

1. Place the carrot in a pan and just cover with boiling water. Bring to the boil then reduce the heat and simmer for 10–15 minutes until cooked. Alternatively, steam for about 15 minutes or until the carrot sticks are cooked.
2. Cool and offer to your baby as a finger food.

a few broccoli florets

1. Place the broccoli in a pan and just cover with boiling water. Bring to the boil then reduce the heat and simmer for about 10 minutes until cooked. Alternatively, steam for about 10 minutes until cooked.
2. Cool and offer to your baby as a finger food.

a small handful of green beans, top and tailed

1. Place the beans in a pan and just cover with boiling water. Bring to the boil then reduce the heat and simmer for 6–8 minutes until cooked. Alternatively, steam for about 6–8 minutes until cooked.
2. Cool and offer to your baby as a finger food.

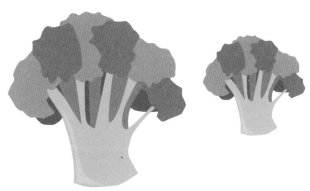

plain rusks
makes 8 small rusks

Although this recipe looks like toast it produces a completely different effect.
The baking of the bread makes it more crumbly in texture which is more palatable
for little ones than toast.

1 slice of wholemeal bread

1. Preheat the oven to 140°C/275°F/Gas Mark 1.
2. Cut the bread into 8 fingers or slices. Place on a baking tray
   and bake in the middle of the oven for 1 hour.
3. Cool and serve.

marmite rusks
makes 8 small rusks

Love it or hate it, Marmite is very strong in flavour and has a high salt content
so use it sparingly. Marmite and wholemeal bread are an excellent source of
the vitamin B group so if your baby likes the combination try sandwiches as
he progresses his diet.

1 slice of wholemeal bread
a little butter
Marmite

1. Preheat the oven to 140°C/275°F/Gas Mark 1.
2. Spread the bread with a little butter and a very small amount
   of Marmite. Cut into 8 fingers or slices. Place on a baking tray
   in the middle of the oven for 1 hour.
3. Cool and serve.

truuuly scrumptious recipes

cheese straws

makes 24

These are an ideal tasty finger food. Cheese is a great source of calcium and vitamin D and the crunchy sesame seeds not only taste great but provide a dose of omega-3, too. If they aren't all eaten whilst still warm (they are difficult to resist), once they are cool pop them in an airtight box and eat within four days.

115 g (4 oz) plain flour
55 g (2 oz) butter, plus extra for greasing
55g (2 oz) mature Cheddar cheese, grated
1 egg, beaten
sesame seeds, for sprinkling (optional)

1 Preheat the oven to 200°C/400°F/gas mark 6. Grease a baking sheet.

2 Sift the flour, then chop the butter into small pieces and add to the flour. Rub together with your fingertips until the mixture resembles breadcrumbs.

3 Add the grated cheese and half the beaten egg mix to form a dough. Wrap in cling film and chill in the fridge for 30 minutes.

4 On a floured work surface roll out the dough to a thickness of 5 mm (¼ in). Cut into strips about 5 cm (2 in) long and 1 cm (½ in) wide and place on the baking sheet. Pinch them together along the sides to give a wavy edge. Brush generously with the remaining egg and sprinkle with sesame seeds, if using.

5 Bake in the oven for 10–15 minutes or until lightly golden. If you cook them for too long they will become dry. Cool and serve.

carrot, courgette & cheese muffins makes 12

These savoury muffins make a delicious nutritious and healthy snack for your baby – and are great for mums and dads, too! Your baby will enjoy tearing the muffin into smaller pieces – just make sure that some of it makes it to his mouth!

225 g (8 oz) self-raising flour
1 tsp baking powder
45 g (1½ oz) butter, plus extra for greasing
115 g (4 oz) mature Cheddar cheese, grated
1 carrot (about 85 g/3 oz), grated
1 small courgette (about 115g/4 oz), grated
½ tsp dried mixed herbs
60 ml (2 fl oz) milk

1 Preheat the oven to 200°C/400°F/gas mark 6. Grease a baking tray with a little butter.

2 Sieve the flour and baking powder into a bowl. Rub in the butter with your fingertips until it resembles breadcrumbs.

3 Add the cheese, carrot, courgette and mixed herbs. Mix in well then add the milk and mix together to form a sticky dough.

4 Knead the dough very lightly on a floured surface then roll into 12 scone shapes and place on the baking tray.

5 Bake in the preheated oven for 15–20 minutes until golden brown. Cool on a wire rack and serve.

6 These muffins freeze well. If you don't want to freeze them, store in an airtight container for 4–5 days.

 truuuly scrumptious recipes

butternut squash & raisin muffins makes 12

These muffins are a great replacement for sweetened snacks, such as cakes and biscuits. The butternut squash and raisins provide the muffins with a sweet flavour so there's no need to add sugar. Older children and adults will eat them as a treat and they won't last long; little do they know they are also good for you, providing vitamin A and fibre!

225 g (8 oz) self-raising flour
1 tsp baking powder
45 g (1½ oz) butter, plus extra for greasing
½ tsp ground cinnamon
½ tsp ground nutmeg
¼ tsp ground ginger
300 g (10½ oz) butternut squash (200 g/7 oz peeled),
*   seeded and grated*
55 g (2 oz) raisins
90 ml (3 fl oz) milk

1 Preheat the oven to 200°C/400°F/gas mark 6. Grease a baking tray with a little butter.

2 Sieve the flour and baking powder into a bowl. Rub in the butter with your fingertips until the mixture resembles breadcrumbs.

3 Add the cinnamon, nutmeg, ginger, butternut squash and raisins. Mix in well then add the milk. Mix together to form a sticky dough.

4 Knead the dough very lightly then roll into 12 scone shapes and place on the baking tray.

5 Bake in the preheated oven for 15–20 minutes until golden brown. Transfer to a wire rack to cool then serve.

6 These are best stored in an airtight container and also freeze well. Be warned, these muffins get eaten within 24 hours in our household – they are very moreish!

fabulous finger foods

apricot oaties makes 15

These are a delicious sugar-free snack and make a great alternative to sugar rusks or biscuits, as they are sweetened with dried apricots which are rich in iron. Remember to use organic apricots which will be darker in colour and do not contain sulphur dioxide. Serve these in between mealtimes or when you are out and about – they're perfect for the whole family.

150 g (5½ oz) oatmeal
¼ tsp bicarbonate of soda
1 tbsp sunflower oil
3 tbsp water

For the apricot purée:
45 g (1½ oz) soft and ready to eat dried organic apricots
(about 6)
75 ml (2½ fl oz) boiling water

1. Preheat the oven to 180°C/350°F/Gas Mark 4.
2. To make the purée, put the apricots and measured boiled water in a pan. Bring to the boil then reduce heat and simmer for 6–8 minutes. Purée in a blender.
3. Put the oatmeal in a mixing bowl and stir in the bicarbonate of soda. Add the puréed apricots and stir well, then stir in the oil.
4. Add the water a tablespoon at a time to form a dough. Allow the dough to rest for a few minutes.
5. Sprinkle your work surface with oatmeal to prevent the dough sticking, and roll the dough out to a thickness of 5 mm (¼ in). Cut into about 15 squares.
6. Place on a baking tray and bake in the centre of the oven for 15–20 minutes.
7. These oaties will keep in an airtight container for up to a week – if they last that long!

truuuly scrumptious recipes

almond butter

makes enough for 4 pieces of toast generously spread

Nut and seed butters are a healthy way to jazz up rice cakes or toast. You could try walnuts, peanuts, cashews, hazelnuts or the larger seeds such as pumpkin or sunflower, or a combination of any of these. Nuts and seeds are a good source of protein and omega-3.

55 g (2 oz) whole unblanched almonds
15 g (½ oz) raisins
2-3 tbsp olive oil

1   Preheat the oven to 180°C/350°F/gas mark 4.
2   Place the almonds on a baking tray on the top shelf of the oven and bake for 10 minutes.
3   Add the roasted almonds, raisins and olive oil to a blender and blend to a smooth purée. You may need to add a little more olive oil to reach the right consistency.
4   Spread on rice cakes or toast – delicious! Store in an airtight container in the fridge for up to two weeks.

suggested menus

weeks 1 and 2

(17 weeks and over)

Breakfast
Breast or bottle

Lunch
Breast or bottle
Baby rice

Tea
Breast or bottle

Bedtime
Breast or bottle

❅

Breakfast
Breast or bottle

Lunch
Breast or bottle
Any single vegetable purée
(see pages 58–60)

Tea
Breast or bottle

Bedtime
Breast or bottle

weeks 3 and 4

(19 weeks and over)

Breakfast
Breast or bottle
Apple purée mixed with baby rice
(see page 69)

Lunch
Breast or bottle
Butternut Squash & Broccoli
(see pages 60–1)

Tea
Breast or bottle

Bedtime
Breast or bottle

❅

Breakfast
Breast or bottle
Peach & Baby Rice (see page 75)

Lunch
Breast or bottle
Sweet Potato, Carrot & Broccoli
(see page 65)

Tea
Breast or bottle

Bedtime
Breast or bottle

weeks 7 and 8

(6–9 months)

Breakfast
Breast or bottle
Apple & Raisin Porridge (see page 117)

Lunch
Milk in a cup
Pasta with Spinach, Watercress & Crème
Fraîche (see page 86)
Seasonal Fruit Compote (see page 122)

Tea
Breast or bottle
Chicken & Winter Vegetable Casserole
(see page 97)

Bedtime
Breast or bottle

Breakfast
Breast or bottle
Baby cereal

Lunch
Milk in a cup
Lentil Bake (see page 85)
Pear, Banana & Apricot (see page 121)

Tea
Breast or bottle
Ratatouille & Quinoa (see page 81)

Bedtime
Breast or bottle

weeks 11 and 12

(9–12 months and over)

Breakfast
Milk in a cup
Weetabix & Pear slices

Lunch
Water in a cup
Lamb & Apricot Casserole (see pages 113–4)
Apples, Blueberries & Quinoa (see pages 123–4)

Tea
Milk in a cup
Pasta with Mushrooms & Butter Beans
(see page 88)
Yoghurt & Mixed Berries (see page 129)

Bedtime
Breast or bottle

Breakfast
Milk in a cup
Banana Porridge (see page 118), toast,
Mango slices

Lunch
Water in a cup
Salmon & Broccoli Pie (see pages 102–3)
Apple, Pear & Kiwi (see page 120)

Tea
Milk in a cup
Sweetcorn Chowder (see page 84)
Coconut Rice Pudding (see page 126)

Bedtime
Breast or bottle

useful contacts

advice on feeding & diets

Allergy UK
3 White Oak Square
London Road
Swanley, Kent
BR8 7AG
Helpline: 01322 619898
www.allergyuk.org
See website for information and advice on allergies.

Association of Breastfeeding Mothers
ABM PO Box 207
Bridgwater, Somerset
TA6 7YT
Helpline: 08444 122949
www.abm.me.uk
For help and support with breastfeeding.

The Breastfeeding Network
PO Box 11126
Paisley, UK
PA2 8YB
Tel: 0870 900 8787
www.breastfeedingnetwork.org.uk
For advice on breastfeeding.

Coeliac UK
Suites A–D Octagon Court
High Wycombe, Bucks
HP11 2HS
Helpline: 0870 444 8804

www.coeliac.co.uk
For advice about gluten intolerance.

The Department of Health
Tel: 020 7210 4850
www.dh.gov.uk
For advice on weaning and other information regarding the health of your baby.

Food Standards Agency
Aviation House
125 Kingsway
London
WC2B 6NH
Tel: 020 7276 8000
www.food.gov.uk
For advice on weaning and other food issues.

The Green Parent magazine
The Green Parent
PO Box 104
East Hoathly, Lewes
BN7 9AX
Tel: 01825 872858
www.thegreenparent.co.uk
Provides information and advice on parenting and green issues.

Janey Lee Grace
www.imperfectlynatural.com
For advice on bringing up your baby in a natural and eco-friendly lifestyle.

La Leche League
PO Box 29
West Bridgford
Nottingham
NG2 7NP
Tel: 0845 456 1855
www.laleche.org.uk
For advice on breastfeeding.

Mumsnet.com
www.mumsnet.com
A great web chat room for mums providing information and parenting advice.

The National Childbirth Trust
Alexandra House
Oldham Terrace
London
W3 6NH
Tel: 0870 444 8707
www.nct.org.uk
For advice on childbirth and local groups.

The Vegan Society
Donald Watson House
21 Hylton Street
Hockley
Birmingham
B18 6HJ
Tel: 0121 523 1730
www.vegansociety.com
Visit the website for advice on vegan diets.

**The Vegetarian Society
of the United Kingdom**
Parkdale
Dunham Road
Altrincham, Cheshire
WA14 4QG
Tel: 0161 925 2000
www.vegsoc.org
*Visit the website for information
regarding vegetarian diets.*

suppliers

Cook Trading Ltd
84 High St
Tonbridge, Kent
TN9 1AP
Home delivery: 0870 870 7338
Other enquiries: 0870 048 9305
www.cookfood.net
*Sell the finest meals, cakes,
puddings and Truuuly Scrumptious
range in their 20 shops and via their
home delivery service.*

Crazy Jack Organic
PO Box 3577
London
NW2 1LQ
www.crazyjack.co.uk
*Crazy Jack produce organic dried
fruit and other ingredients.*

FARMA
12 Southgate Street
Winchester,
Hampshire
SO23 9EF
Tel: 0845 4588 420
www.farma.org.uk
*To find out information regarding
farmers markets or farm shops.*

Graig Farm Organics
Dolau
Llandrindod Wells, Powys
LD1 5TL
Tel: 01597 851655
www.graigfarm.co.uk
*Graig Farm offer home delivery
for organic meat and a variety
of products including Truuuly
Scrumptious.*

John Lewis
Tel: 08456 049 049
www.johnlewis.com
For feeding and cooking equipment.

Mothercare
Tel: 08453 30 40 70
www.mothercare.com
For feeding equipment.

Olimia Ltd
1B Church Street
Reigate, Surrey
RH2 0AA
Tel: 01737 233551
www.olimia.com
*Olimia offer home delivery for
natural pregnancy and baby
products including the Truuuly
Scrumptious range.*

Organix Brands Ltd
Freepost BH1 336
Christchurch, Dorset
BH23 2ZZ
Tel: 0800 39 35 11
www.organix.com
*Organix produce a fantastic
range of organic food for
babies and toddlers.*

**Riverford Organic
Vegetables Ltd**
Wash Barn

Buckfastleigh, Devon
TQ11 0LD
Tel: 01803 762720
www.riverford.co.uk
Provide home delivery of
organic fruit and vegetables.

Sheepdrove Organic Farm
Warren Farm
Lambourn, Berkshire
RG17 7UU
Tel: 01488 674747
www.sheepdroveshop.com
*Sheepdrove offer home
delivery of organic meat.*

Soil Association
South Plaza
Marlborough Street
Bristol
BS1 3NX
Tel: 0117 314 5000
www.soilassociation.org
*See the website for more
information on organic food
or sourcing foods.*

Soil Association Scotland
18 Liberton Brae
Tower Mains
Edinburgh
EH16 6AE
Tel: 0131 666 2474
www.soilassociation.org

Truuuly Scrumptious
Office 1
Edford Rural Business Park
Edford Farm
Edford Hill
Holcombe, Radstock
BA3 5HQ
Tel: 01761 239300
www.bathorganicbabyfood.co.uk

index

index 143

1 3 5 7 9 10 8 6 4 2

Published in 2008 by Vermilion, an imprint of
Ebury Publishing

A Random House Group Company

The Random House Group Limited Reg. No. 954009

Addresses for companies within the Random House
Group can be found at

www.randomhouse.co.uk

A CIP catalogue record for this book is available from the
British Library

The Random House Group Limited makes every effort to
ensure that the papers used in our books are made from
trees that have been legally sourced from well-managed
and credibly certified forests. Our paper procurement
policy can be found on www.rbooks.co.uk/environment

To buy books by your favourite authors and register for
offers visit www.rbooks.co.uk

Designed by Smith & Gilmour, London

Printed and bound in Singapore by Tien Wah Press

ISBN 9780091922054

Please note that conversions to imperial weights
and measures are suitable equivalents and not exact.

The information given in this book should not be treated
as a substitute for qualified medical advice; always consult
a medical practitioner. Neither the author nor the publisher
can be held responsible for any loss or claim arising out of
the use, or misuse, of the suggestions made or the failure
to take medical advice.